Foreword

They published *The Unpublished David Ogilvy* on David's seventy-fifth birthday in 1986, and gave it to him at a boat party in London. (At the time I was slaving as a Junior Account Director in our offices at Brettenham House by Waterloo Bridge and blithely ignorant of the doings of the Great and the Good Salon on the river below).

Ken Roman was Ogilvy & Mather's CEO at the time and it was his idea to begin with. Then it was Bill Phillips, another CEO, who enabled it. Bill wrote the original Foreword and I am honored to follow on over twenty-five years later. Bill wrote at the time that, when David received his copy, "for once, words failed him."

Otherwise, words were what made him. Reading this collection, one is struck, piece after piece, whether in the most apparently (but perhaps not so) casual of memoranda or the most public of pronouncements, by how David's words surprise and seduce, tease and provoke.

To me, his writing is in the best tradition of Dr. Johnson – opinionated, forceful and urgent, whether it addresses the higher principles of management or the dangers of the lowly paper clip. Above all, though, one can see in it the recurring theme of his love for people, which is an abiding legacy for us in Ogilvy & Mather and an essential part of the extraordinary culture which he crafted and which endures so strongly.

David and Herta Ogilvy at Touffou, their home in France, in June 1986.

When Ken and Bill decided to make this book, they turned to Joel Raphaelson, one of David's paladins. I asked Joel how he went about it and this is what he told me.

"I canvassed the Ogilvy world, asking for anything David had written, handwritten or typed, long or short, important and thoughtful or spontaneous and frivolous. Responses by the dozen came pouring into my office in Chicago. When I'd accumulated a big stack I went through it, item by item, hoping to find things piling up naturally into a few well-defined categories. And they did. For example, I saw to my surprise that I'd made a pile of memos made up entirely of lists."

But perhaps Joel's most important contribution was getting the money to pay for David's court typographer, Ingeborg Baton, to leave retirement, and her native Denmark, in order to design the typography. In Joel's words, "that made sure the result would be something that would please David to look at. The relaxed good looks of the book are thanks to her."

Relaxed though this book may be, it will also stimulate the most jaded brain in today's world of business, different in so many degrees – but not in fundamental kind – to the years when David was building his first-class business in a first-class way.

It very well deserves this re-publishing.

Miles Young
Worldwide Chairman and CEO, Ogilvy & Mather
September 2012

In 1971, on the ranch in Argentina where his father was born

Contents

Aged 27.

Early Years

Early Years

In 1936, as a 25-year-old assistant account executive, David somehow was given the entire staff of his agency as an audience for his views on advertising. He came across his pronunciamento years later, when he was Chairman of Ogilvy & Mather, and sent the following excerpt to his Board, commenting that "it proves two things: A) At 25 I was brilliantly clever, and B) I have learned nothing new in the subsequent 27 years."

Every advertisement must tell the whole sales story, because the public does not read advertisements in series.

The copy must be human and very simple, keyed right down to its market – a market in which self-conscious artwork and fine language serve only to make buyers wary.

Every word in the copy must count. Concrete figures must be substituted for atmospheric claims; clichés must give way to facts, and empty exhortations to alluring offers.

Facetiousness in advertising is a device dear to the amateur but anathema to the advertising agent, who knows that permanent success has rarely been built on frivolity and that people do not buy from clowns.

Superlatives belong to the marketplace and have no place in a serious advertisement; they lead readers to discount the realism of every claim.

Apparent monotony of treatment must be tolerated, because only the manufacturer reads all his own advertisements.

•   •   •

From "The Theory & Practice of Selling the Aga Cooker," a guide for his fellow door-to-door salesmen written in 1935 when David was twenty-four years old.

In an article about him in 1971, Fortune *called it "probably the best sales manual ever written."*

Much of what it espoused for selling stoves door-to-door can be put to good use a half-century later for selling any kind of goods in any medium.

FOREWORD

In Great Britain, there are twelve million households. One million of these own motorcars. Only ten thousand own Aga Cookers. No household which can afford a motorcar can afford to be without an Aga ...

There are certain universal rules. Dress quietly and shave well. Do not wear a bowler hat. Go to the back door (most salesmen go to the front door, a manoeuvre always resented by maid and mistress alike) ... Tell the person who opens the door frankly and briefly what you have come for; it will get her on your side. Never on any account get in on false pretences.

Study the best time of day for calling; between twelve and two p.m. you will not be welcome, whereas a call at an unorthodox time of day – after supper in the summer for instance – will often succeed ... In general, study the methods of your competitors and do the exact opposite.

Find out all you can about your prospects before you call on them; their general living conditions, wealth, profession, hobbies, friends and so on. Every hour spent in this kind of research will help you and impress your prospect ...

The worst fault a salesman can commit is to be a bore ... Pretend to be vastly interested in any subject the prospect shows an interest in. The more she talks the better, and if you can make her laugh you are several points up ...

Perhaps the most important thing of all is to avoid standardisation in your sales talk. If you find yourself one fine day saying the same things to a bishop and a trapezist, you are done for.

When the prospect tries to bring the interview to a close, go gracefully. It can only hurt you to be kicked out ...

The more prospects you talk to, the more sales you expose yourself to, the more orders you will get. But never mistake quantity of calls for quality of salesmanship.

Quality of salesmanship involves energy, time and knowledge of the product ... We may analyse it under two main headings, ATTACK AND DEFENCE ...

ATTACK

1. **GENERAL STATEMENT**. Most people have heard

something about the Aga Cooker. They vaguely believe it to involve some new method of cooking. They may have heard that it works on the principle of "heat storage." Heat storage is the oldest known form of cooking. Aborigines bake their hedgehogs in the ashes of a dying fire ...

Having got some preliminary remarks ... off your chest, find out as quickly as possible which of the particular sales arguments that follow is most likely to appeal to your audience, and give that argument appropriate emphasis. Stockbrokers will appreciate No. 2. Doctors will understand No. 9. Cooks will be won over with No. 5. Only on rare occasions will you have the opportunity of getting through all twelve arguments.

2. ECONOMY. The Aga is the only cooker in the world with a guaranteed maximum fuel consumption. It is guaranteed to burn less than £4 worth of fuel a year ...

Stress the fact that no cook can make her Aga burn more fuel than this, however stupid, extravagant or careless she may be, or however much she may cook. If more fuel is consumed, it is being stolen, and the police should be called in immediately ...

3. ALWAYS READY. You cannot surprise an Aga. It is always on its toes, ready for immediate use at any time of the day or night. It is difficult for a cook or housewife who has not known an Aga to realise exactly what this will mean to her. Tell her she can come down in the middle of the night and roast a goose, or even refill her hot water bottle ... Hot breakfast may be given to the wretched visitor who has to start back to London at zero hour on Monday morning.

On the boat emigrating to America, 1938.

4. CLEANLINESS, with which may be coupled beauty, is a virtue sometimes better appreciated by the prospect than by the salesman. The woman who does the work in a house spends more time on cleaning than on anything else …

The Aga is innately clean … Ladies can cook a dinner on the Aga in evening dress. Doctors will agree that it is so clean that it would not look out of place in the sterilising room of an operating theatre …

An occasional flowery phase is called for to allow your enthusiasm full scope in describing the beauty and cleanliness of the Aga. Think some up and produce them *extempore*.

5. **COOKERY**. It is hopeless to try and sell a single Aga unless you know something about cookery and appear to know more than you actually do. It is not simply a question of knowing which part of the Aga bakes and which simmers. You must be able to talk to cooks and housewives on their own ground ...

Aga grilling should be featured, particularly to men, who are almost always interested in this if in no other method of cooking; it is the only culinary operation they ever see and understand ...

The Roasting Oven. Learn to recognise vegetarians on sight. It is painful indeed to gush over roasting and grilling to a dropping face which has not enjoyed the pleasures of a beefsteak for several years.

Before you open the top oven door, either actually or by description, forestall the inevitable observation that it "looks very small." It is an optical illusion ... Demonstrate with exaggerated groping how far back the oven goes ...

Baking interests most women more than roasting. Without beating about the bush, tell the prospect that pastry baking, bread baking and cake baking are star turns ... Most women are subject to baking fits, and the ability to give this idiosyncracy full rein may be enlarged upon at length ...

Casseroles and stews – luxuries where the gas or

MODESTY

David gave a talk to the Bombay Advertising Club in 1982. Afterward he was asked: "Mr. Ogilvy, Indian advertising draws its inspiration from Madison Avenue. What about Madison Avenue? What is its source?"

The reply: "Modesty forbids."

---

electricity bill has to be remembered – become the master passion of the Aga cook. Stock, ham, and porridge cook all night long and lose their terrors for the dyspeptic. Cure the world of stomachache and heartburn – what a mission!

6. **APPEAL TO COOKS.** If there is a cook in the house, she is bound to have the casting vote over a new cooker. Butter her up. Never go above her head. Before the sale and afterwards as a user a cook can be your bitterest enemy or your best friend; she can poison a whole district or act as your secret representative. The Aga will mean for her an extra hour in bed, and a kitchen as clean as a drawing-room …

7. **APPEAL TO MEN.** When selling to men who employ a staff or whose wives do their cooking, make a discreet appeal to their humane instincts. The Aga takes the slavery out of kitchen work. It does not cook the cook.

And compare the prices! If you can work on this appeal to a man's better nature and combine it with an appeal to his pocket and his belly, you cannot fail to secure an order …

8. **APPEAL TO SPECIAL CLASSES**. Children can be given the run of the Aga kitchen for making toffee and so on. There is no danger of burning, electric shocks, gassing or explosion.

Doctors will admire your perspicacity if you tell them that ... if a case keeps them long after the normal hour for dinner they will get an unspoilt meal on their return to an Aga house ...

There is no end to the special appeal Aga has for every conceivable class and profession. Think it out.

9. **SUMMARY OF MISCELLANEOUS ECONOMIES**. The Aga means fuel saving, staff reduction, reduced expenditure on cleaning materials, reduction of meat shrinkage and food wastage, abolition of chimney-sweeps; painting and redecorating is unheard of; electric irons and their antics are unnecessary; raids on registry offices for new servants become a thing of the past; the house can be let or sold at any time on its kitchen; bilious attacks and doctor's bills are halved; restaurants are seldom visited, and, as the French say: "The Aga owner eats best at home."

10. **WISE-CRACKING**. The longer you talk to a prospect, the better, and you will not do this if you are a bore. Pepper your talk with anecdote and jokes. Accumulate a repertoire of illustration. Above all, laugh till you cry every time the prospect makes the joke about the Aga Khan. A deadly serious demonstration is bound to fail. If you can't make a lady laugh, you certainly cannot make her buy.

DEFENCE

1. **GENERAL ADVICE**. You must always be faced soon or later with questions and objections, which may indeed be taken as a sign that the prospect's brain is in working order, and that she is conscientiously considering the Aga as a practical proposition for herself.

Some salesmen expound their subject academically, so that at the end the prospect feels no more inclination to buy the Aga than she would to buy the planet Jupiter after a broadcast from the Astronomer Royal. A talkative prospect is a good thing. The dumb prospect is too often equally deaf ...

2. **DETAILED OBJECTIONS.**

"It is too big for my kitchen."

Boloney always. It only looks big because it does not, like gas stoves, stand on legs. Make the objection a pretext for going into the kitchen to measure, and continue the conversation there ...

Continue: There is no danger of getting burned with an Aga, so that it is possible to go right up to it. You have to give a range a very wide berth ...

"Can the Aga give off unpleasant fumes?"

The flue construction makes this quite impossible; a striking manifestation of the inventor's genius. [You will sometimes come across people with unfortunate gassing experiences of closed stoves. Try and avoid the subject as it introduces the wrong atmosphere.]

"Can the Aga make toast?"

Extremely well ... To the prospect who has positive information that her neighbour's Aga makes toast like white tiles, admit that the old Aga was rather weak in this regard; the present cooker is so fast that it toasts diabolically well.

"Does the smell of food cooking on the Aga penetrate all over the house?"

Nothing so impolite. The ovens ventilate direct into the flue so that all cooking smells are dispersed up the chimney. How different from ordinary ovens, which irresponsibly discharge their perfume into the kitchen.

"My cooker *must* heat the bath water as well."

Explain that, as somebody with experience of heating engineering, you would strongly advise one heat unit for cooking and another separate unit for hot water; to combine the two units results inevitably in outrageous fuel consumption, and that kind of Victorian inefficiency means hot bath and cold oven, or hot oven and cold bath.

Continue: The Aga is called a "Cooker." And, by heaven, that is what it is! Off you go again on the cooking advantages.

"I have heard of somebody who is dissatisfied."

Probably at second hand. These malicious reports are spread by jealous people who have not got an Aga. Express grave concern and try to find out the name and address so that you can rush away then and there to put matters right. In this way you will give the prospect a foretaste of willing service.

Clearing the orchard on the farm in Pennsylvania in 1947.

Continue: Do you know so-and-so, who has just put in an Aga? Go on mentioning all the satisfied owners in the district until you find someone whose name is familiar to the prospect.

3. **COMPETITORS**. Try and avoid being drawn into discussing competitive makes of cooker, as it introduces a negative and defensive atmosphere. On no account sling mud – it can carry very little weight, coming from you, and it will make the prospect distrust your integrity and dislike you.

The best way to tackle the problem is to find out all you possibly can about the merits, faults and sales

ECCENTRICITIES

When Ken Brady became the head of Ogilvy & Mather in Jakarta at twenty-nine, he received a note from David saying, "You're a remarkable young man. Please come to New York so I can shake your hand."

In due course Ken turned up in David's office, where he received this advice:

"Develop your eccentricities while you're young. That way, when you get old, people won't think you're going gaga."

arguments of competitors, and then keep quiet about them. Profound knowledge of other cookers will help you put your positive case for Aga more convincingly …

4. **PRICE DEFENCE**. It pays to approach this subject off your own bat and in your own time … But sooner or later a prospect will ask you the price before you are ready. The way to reply is the supreme test of your salesmanship. Your voice, your manner, your expression, even your smell, must be controlled and directed to soften the blow …

The way you continue the conversation after announcing the price is of great importance. It is no use fatuously remarking that it is "not really expensive." You must be specific, definite and factual. The prospect is not interested in your personal opinion as to what is or is not expensive for her.

The following suggestions will give you an indication

of the kind of way to cope with the reactions of different prospects to the price announcement:-

"It is too much money for me."

A famous surgeon was once asked by a friend how much he had charged a very poor patient for removing his appendix. "A hundred pounds," the surgeon replied. "But how much had he?" asked his friend. "A hundred pounds," replied the surgeon. Most Aga prospects have got £47 10s. If you can't get it someone else will.

"The price will come down."

If you wait a year, and even if the price did come down (which it won't), you will still be out of pocket by another year's fuel consumption.

Continue: The Aga will never be mass-produced; like a Rolls-Royce it is too good for mass production. If you could buy a Rolls which was so economical in fuel that it did 2,000 miles to a gallon of petrol, what would you be willing to pay for such a car? The analogy is a close one.

"We are getting old. It would not pay us."

Old cooks and housewives need an Aga more than young ones. And don't forget that the Aga increases expectation of life.

People come to live life more and more in the house as they grow old. A house which is smoothly run means everything to old people, and food comes to play an increasingly important part in their lives as death approaches. And what an heirloom!

Continue: The Aga promotes digestion ...

In 1945 David developed a "Plan for a Company of Merchant Adventurers to Engage in the Export & Import Business Between the United Kingdom and the Western Hemisphere." Here is one section:

March 25, 1945

A British Advertising Agency in the Western Hemisphere

No British advertising agency has a branch anywhere in the Western Hemisphere. The export drive would be strengthened if a British agency opened offices in New York, Rio, Buenos Aires.

The largest advertising agency in London is the branch of an American agency. Before the war their turnover was approximately £2,000,000 per annum. There were at least six other American agencies in London. They helped to launch on the British market such American products as PEPSODENT, WRIGLEY'S, LISTERINE, QUAKER OATS, POND'S, ESSO, PALMOLIVE. They can claim part of the credit for the fact that the visible balance of trade was $400,000,000 in America's favor.

But there was no British advertising agency in the U.S. No British agency had the enterprise to emulate the example of its American competitors.

It is proposed that we should consider participating in the establishment of a British advertising agency in New York, Rio and Buenos Aires. The most convenient procedure would be to tie up with one of the existing London agencies: Mather & Crowther.

Our agency would have three main functions:

(1) To advertise the products imported by our trading subsidiaries.

(2) To offer local advertisers and agencies consultative advice on the British market. Fee basis. Help local agencies with British copy angles.

(3) To place American advertising in America, i.e., to become a full-fledged American agency. It would be possible at the start to hire one or two men who could *bring with them* enough American business to take care of a considerable part of our overhead.

Reflecting on this in 1986, David said that "the Company of Merchant Adventurers came into being and prospered, but it did not start the advertising agency, so I resigned and started it myself."

At work in the early 1950s.

Notes, Memos, and Letters

Notes, Memos, and Letters

An autobiographical note to Bill Phillips:

March 5, 1971

Will Any Agency Hire This Man?

He is 38, and unemployed. He dropped out of college. He has been a cook, a salesman, a diplomatist and a farmer. He knows nothing about marketing, and has never written any copy. He professes to be interested in advertising as a career (at the age of 38!) and is ready to go to work for $5,000 a year.

I doubt if any American agency will hire him.

However, a London agency *did* hire him. Three years later he became the most famous copywriter in the world, and in due course built the tenth biggest agency in the world.

The moral: it sometimes pay an agency to be imaginative and unorthodox in hiring.

D.O.

From a memo to the Board:

December 8, 1971

Gentlemen – With Brains

In *Principles of Management* I said, "One of the most priceless assets Ogilvy & Mather can have is the *respect* of our clients and the whole business community."

With every passing year, I am increasingly impressed with the truth of this.

It is not enough for an agency to be respected for its professional competence. Indeed, there isn't much to choose between the competence of the big agencies.

What so often makes the difference is the character of the men and women who represent the agency at the top level, with clients and the business community.

If they are respected as admirable people, the agency gets business – whether from present clients or prospective ones. (I am coming to think that it also counts with the investment community.)

… John Loudon recently told me, "In choosing men to head countries for Shell, I have always thought that *character* is the most important thing of all."

Ogilvy & Mather must have "gentlemen with brains" – not only in London and New York, but in *all* our countries.

To compromise with this principle sometimes looks expedient, short term. But it can never do Ogilvy & Mather any permanent good.

D.O.

P.S. By "gentlemen" I do not, of course, mean Old Etonians and all that.

• • •

A note to heads of offices:

January 4, 1980

Year after year, I see the creative output of every office. Year after year, I also see their profits.

My conclusion: "The better the advertising, the more profitable the office. The worse the advertising, the more money the office loses."

David Ogilvy

• • •

A memo that struck terror into the hearts of the agency's eleven copywriters, written when David decided, on the departure of Jud Irish, to become Copy Chief himself:

August 15, 1959

In my new role as Copy Chief, it will be necessary for me to know more about the talents of our copywriters than I now know.

Will you please let me see – in proof or layout form – the six best advertisements (print or broadcast) that you have produced since joining Ogilvy, Benson & Mather, and the three best that you had produced in your previous incarnations – if any.

I would like to have these on my desk before tomorrow evening.

David Ogilvy

• • •

A reference letter for Dave McCall, a former Copy Chief of Ogilvy, Benson & Mather:

February 28, 1964

Dear Mr. Weis:

Mr. McCall is an old friend of mine. He joined our company twelve years ago. When he resigned he was a Director and Senior Vice-President.

He and his family are splendid in every way – in spite of the fact that he is white, a Republican and a Christian.

Yours Truly,

D.O.

• • •

A letter to the New Hampshire Vacation Center:

April 12, 1971

Gentlemen:

"America is alive and well and living in New Hampshire." This is one of the best headlines I have ever read.

I offer humble congratulations to the man or woman who wrote it.

Yours sincerely,

D.O.

To Cliff Field, a great copywriter, on his seventh anniversary with the company:

September 21, 1963

Cliff:

I see that you have been here for seven years. I've been here for twice as long. God knows what this proves.

D.O.

•   •   •

From a letter to Geoff Lindley, later head of Ogilvy & Mather in Sydney, when Geoff was in New Zealand:

Dear Geoff,

Your Status Reports always make good reading, for a lot of reasons. The one dated April 22nd is no exception.

I love the fact that we are to advertise "a silent flushing system." Your copywriter may be able to do something with the fact that Queen Victoria bestowed a knighthood on a man who had advanced the art of flushing. His name was Sir Thomas Crapper.

I also enjoy reading about "the wig sell-in." What an extraordinary business we are …

A memo to the Board:

October 11, 1978

A Teaching Hospital

I have a new metaphor.

Great hospitals do two things: They look after patients, and they teach young doctors.

Ogilvy & Mather does two things: We look after clients, and we teach young advertising people.

Ogilvy & Mather is the teaching hospital of the advertising world. And, as such, to be respected above all other agencies.

I prefer this to Stanley Resor's old saying that J. Walter Thompson was a "university of advertising."

D.O.

•　•　•

A note to Cliff Field who at the time was Creative Head of the agency:

June 11, 1965

Cliff:

_____ thinks that this is a great advertisement. I don't. *It lacks charm.*

It plods. Heavy as lead. The models – most of them – look like automobile dealers from South Dakota. Not the way to capture the affections of the people who read *The New Yorker*.

I plead for charm, flair, showmanship, taste, distinction.

D.O.

A memo to the New York office's seven "Syndicate Heads," as David dubbed the leaders of his creative groups:

April 29, 1971

A Word to the Wise

Long ago I realized that I lack competence, or interest, or both, in several areas of our business. Notably television programming, finance, administration, commercial production and marketing.

So I hired people who are strong in those areas where I am weak.

Every one of you Syndicate Heads is strong in some areas, weak in others. Take my advice: get people alongside you who make up for your weaknesses.

If you are strong in production and weak in strategy, have a strategist as your right arm.

If you are strong on strategy and weak in production, have a production genius as your right arm.

If your taste is uncertain – or nonexistent – have someone at your right hand whose taste is impeccable.

If you are a print writer and inept in television, get someone beside you who is the reverse. (Some of you are good at TV but haven't a clue about print.)

If you are weak in package goods, have someone at your right hand who is strong in this area.

* * * * *

Don't compound your own weaknesses by employing people in key positions who have the *same* weakness.

* * * * *

Who wants to admit, even to himself, that he has no taste, or is bored by television production, or inadequate on strategy?

Ah, that is the question.

One of the recipients of this memo responded by asking David's advice on what sort of people he should hire. Here are excerpts from a long, handwritten reply:

June 9, 1971

Dear _____

You are the *only* one of the Syndicate Heads who has asked me this question. Which says a lot about you …

It would be easier for me to answer the question *specifically* for certain other Syndicate Heads:

A   has terrible taste, so should get someone who has good taste

B   is a mere execution man – he should get a strategist

C   is blind to graphics and so are his art
     directors

D   ditto

E   is a shit and should hire an angel

I am making a speech next week to the grand American Chamber of Commerce in London. I'm so nervous that I'm having nightmares about it.

                                    Yours,

                                    David

A trait that sometimes surprised newcomers to the Agency was the attention David directed to the smallest details of people's jobs, as in this memo to account supervisors ad account executives:

                                    May 8, 1958

              How to Be Helpful at Meetings

Every week we have several meetings – with clients, and among ourselves. Most of the talking at these meetings is apt to be done by the most senior people present. This sometimes leaves the junior people with nothing to do except listen.

Anyway, that seems to be the general idea. But it is wrong. First of all, junior people should not hesitate to speak out. For example, if they disagree with something I am saying, they should say so – before it is too late. Very often, I lack information which is available to them.

But the main purpose of this memo is to say that the most junior agency representative present at any meeting *should make himself useful by "servicing" the meeting*.

For example, if we start discussing an old advertisement, he should leave the room and return with the advertisement. Then we would have it before us and could discuss it more sensibly.

If at some point in the meeting it becomes apparent that we would make more progress if we had the art director or one of the media experts present, the junior man should leave the meeting and return with the person concerned.

All too often I see our junior people sitting on their fannies, not reacting to the stimuli which arise ...

Above all, it is true to say that the success of a meeting often depends on having the right documents – proofs, artwork, schedules, research charts, etc. – present at the start of the meeting. All too often we arrive like plumbers, leaving our tools behind.

D.O.

• • •

A memo to the staff, sent out every eighteen months or so during the early years of the company:

March 22, 1957

The paper clip is a very dangerous instrument. When it is used to fasten papers together, it frequently picks up a paper which doesn't belong. And it frequently drops a paper which does belong.

All offices, including this one, have lost very valuable papers because of these wretched little clips.

In circulating papers around our offices here, please use these clips as little as possible. It is much safer and more efficient to use a stapler; or, if papers are too bulky for a stapler, use the binder clips.

• • •

A handwritten note to Joel Raphaelson, undated, but probably during 1964:

Joel:

I thought you promised to show me the Shears ads (with copy) last Tuesday.

It is now three months since Struthers picked them. Longer than the period of gestation in PIGS.

D.O.

  ⚲   ⚲   ⚲

A letter to Ray Taylor, a former Ogilvy & Mather copywriter, on his retirement, from another agency:

June 29, 1983

Dear Ray:

Nineteen years ago you wrote me the best job application letter I have ever received. I can still recite the first paragraph.*

---

*Editor's note: The first paragraph read: "My father was in charge of the men's lavatory at the Ritz Hotel. My mother was a chambermaid at the same hotel. I was educated at the London School of Economics."

For the next three years you were one of the best copywriters ever employed in our New York office.

I was miserable when you returned to London, and still more miserable when you joined another agency.

But I cannot grudge Masius their good fortune in recruiting you, because it was Mike Masius who got me my first job in the United States.

Now I hear that you are retiring. What a waste of genius.

May your shadow never grow less.

Yours affectionately,

David Ogilvy

֍ ֍ ֍

A letter to Peter Warren, Chairman of Ogilvy & Mather in the United Kingdom.

May 15, 1983

Dear Peter,

It was very good of you to send me Lord Denning's book. I finished reading it last night.

What a curious way of writing. I have often been accused of writing too staccato, but compared with Denning, I am positively long-winded.

A draper begot a General, an Admiral and a Judge. I know of a similar case. A poor coal merchant in Invernesshire, who carried his coal into his customers' houses on his back, begot a General, a Judge and a Cabinet Minister.

Marvelous.

Yours,

David

❦   ❦   ❦

A note to Jackie Kilgour, who was putting together an annual report, about which of two photographs to use:

JK:

I like (A) better because it makes me look YOUNGER and NICER. But no man should be allowed to pick his own photo. So I defer to your judgment.

D.O.

• • •

A comment about the paper clips David uses to secure his neckties inspired this memo to Michael Ball, then a Vice Chairman.

July 15, 1981

TIE CLIPS

Some people are *naturally* extravagant – with their own money and the company's money.

I believe that it would increase profits if the Barons* would *inculcate a tradition of parsimony throughout their archdioceses*. (Some of the Barons are themselves extravagant.)

How to do it? Here are some ideas:

(1) Crack down publicly on two or three office heads who spend too much on *decorating their offices*.

(2) Wage war on the unnecessary use of telex. I have the impression that telex has become the normal medium for interoffice communication, as it is in the Diplomatic Service. The vast majority of telex messages I see are not urgent in any way.

For example, _____'s 500-word telex about awards. Not long ago, _____ sent me an even longer and even less urgent telex.

I find extravagance esthetically repulsive. I find the New England Puritan tradition more attractive. And more profitable.

It is a matter of posture, manners, style and *habit*.

* * * * *

People see the telex machine in their offices. It looks like a typewriter. Maybe they think it is *free* …

David

---

*Regional directors.

The guilty Junkers – or one just like it.

LOSES TASTE FOR FLYING

Why doesn't David like to *fly*? In a 1985 interview in *Resume*, a Swedish magazine, he told this story:

> "Everything began one beautiful summer evening in Stockholm in the 1930's. I was on a cruise, but when I arrived late back to the harbour one evening the boat had already left. There was no alternative but to fly to Helsinki. The plane was a three-engined Junkers which bounced about in appalling turbulence. I felt terrible and lost my taste for flying for life ..."

Advances in aviation technology leave him skeptical. "Turbulence is what frightens me" begins a recent note to Vice Chairman James Benson. "Is there more or less of it on the Concorde?"

David likes to remind his partners of the economies he achieves by living in a château in France, as in this memo to seven senior people in the United States and the United Kingdom:

August 7, 1969

FRENCH PRICES – OUTSIDE PARIS

The other night I gave a dinner for nine at a restaurant near Touffou. We had several courses, and five bottles of wine. The bill was $31.00 or £13.

D.O.

A memo to Ogilvy & Mather Directors about Warren Buffett, Chairman of Berkshire-Hathaway and one of the most perspicacious investors in the United States:

April 4, 1983

How to Make Money Out of Ogilvy & Mather

Warren Buffett has made a profit of $15,400,000 on his Ogilvy & Mather stock – so far.

He and his foundation have 401,400 shares, for which he paid an average of $9.47.

D.O.

Shelby Page, the agency's Treasurer for thirty-six years, received a telex from France shortly after Mitterand was elected. Here's the whole telex:

From: *David Ogilvy*

To: *Shelby Page*

Mitterand is going to tax the rich.

I am rich.

* * * * *

To Luis Muñoz-Marin, former Governor of Puerto Rico, and architect of Puerto Rico's relationship with the U.S., after his party was returned to power in the 1972 elections:

November 21, 1972

Dear Governor:

Thank God.

Yours ever,

D.O.

The opening of a report to his partner on a tour of offices in New Zealand, Australia and Southeast Asia:

April 1, 1978

Down Under

We set sail from Acapulco in QE2 on January 27, bound for New Zealand. Most of our fellow passengers were rich octogenarians with stentorian voices. One woman had brought sixty-nine evening dresses. Much to the chagrin of the tip-hungry waiters, six or seven of our senile shipmates died every day and were buried at sea – discreetly, at five o'clock in the morning, with the ship hove to so that they would not be mashed by the propellers. Cheap, as funerals go ...

Alas, we did not call in the New Hebrides, a group of islands which are ruled by France and Britain jointly. Portraits of the Queen and the President of France hang side by side in every public place. The inhabitants understand who the *Queen* is, and assume that the other portrait is her *King*; they notice with interest that she changes kings every six years.

We fell in love with New Zealand – a society without class distinctions, thousands of small yachts in every harbor, beautifully kept gardens, and magnificent scenery. Here began the promotional whirlwind in which we have lived ever since ...

Answering a skeptical question as to the truth of a story he tells about the bizarre results of a certain advertisement, David scribbled this note:

I made it up, years ago.

Poetic license. It always gets a laugh.

So shut up.

* * * * *

A memo to a veteran copywriter:

April 2, 1971

Harry has just read me the letter you wrote me yesterday, on your anniversary.

Shyness makes it impossible for me to tell any man what I think of him when he is still alive. However, if I outlive you, I shall write an obituary along these lines:

_____ was probably the nicest man I have ever known. His kindness to me, and to dozens of other people, was nothing short of angelic.

Many nice men are too dumb to be anything else. But _____ was far from dumb. Indeed, he had a superb intelligence.

His judgment of men and events was infallible; I came to rely on it more and more as the years went by.

He was one of my few partners who worked

harder and longer hours than I did. He gave value for money. And he knew his trade.

He was an honest man, in the largest sense of the word. He had a glorious sense of humor.

He had the courage to challenge me when he thought I was wrong, but he always contrived to do it without annoying me.

There was nothing saccharine about him. Tolerant as he was, he did not like *everybody*; he disliked the people who deserved to be disliked.

He never pursued popularity, but he inspired universal affection.

I cannot sign this, because I am in Chicago and it will have to be typed in New York ...

❨ ❨ ❨

A memo to Alex Biel, head of the Ogilvy Center for Research and Development, in response to a suggestion that the Center publish a newsletter:

April 26, 1985

ALEX BIEL

If *you* think this is a good idea, far be it from me to stop you. But consider:

1. Our heads of office are *drowning* in paper.

2. We hired you to do pioneer, basic research – not to issue newsletters.

3. We have too many newsletters already.

4. Can you imagine Einstein issuing "What's new in research" memos?

D.O.

   ❦   ❦   ❦

A later memo to Alex Biel:

September 12, 1985

DISLIKES

In your memo of August 1 to Jack, you wrote, "Most people simply do not dislike commercials."

When I was doing research for Hollywood, I found that most people did not dislike *any* movie stars.

Forty-five years ago I came to the conclusion that ordinary Americans are too nice, or too dumb, or too passive, or too uncritical to dislike *anything*.

D.O.

From a 1982 memo to Hank Bernhard, former Vice-Chairman of Ogilvy & Mather, U.S.:

Surface Hypnotism

Anyone who used to watch the Candid Camera show on television must have been surprised by Alan Funt's ability to get people to do anything he wanted them to do. He simply *told them to do it* and they did. Surface hypnotism?

Before a recent speech in Los Angeles, I signaled to the audience with my hands to *stand up*. To my surprise, they stood up – all 1200 of them – and gave me a standing ovation.

D.O.

* * * * *

A chatty letter on several subjects, to John Straiton, former President of Ogilvy & Mather in Canada, began with a paragraph about a departed colleague:

Eating cheese at dinner has always given me terrible nightmares. Last night I ate a cheese fondue at a dinner in Switzerland – and dreamed that _____ was back in the agency.

Two notes to Joel Raphaelson:

July 27, 1982

I have come across a fascinating word. It means "the first rudiments" of anything. In the big Oxford dictionary. Various spellings:

ABECEDARY

ABCEDARIE

ABSCEDARY

Perhaps too obscure for use in headlines.

D.O.

* * * * *

December 14, 1984

Joel:

"He got in his LIMO and drove to his CONDO." I don't think the language is improving.

D.O.

A note to Alex Biel – from an exchange about jargon:

May 15, 1985

ENGLISH

A brand manager who recently left told the agency that he was pursuing a policy of

PRE-EMPTIVE DIMENSIONALIZATION OF BETTERMENT.

D.O.

§ § §

David sends around a lot of clippings, with notes attached. One such clipping was a headline in the International Herald Tribune:

SUSLOV, 79, DIES: KREMLIN IDEOLOGIST

Top Guardian of Communist Dogma

Succumbs After "Brief, Grave Illness"

The attached note:

Damn right the illness was "grave"

– it *killed* him.

A note to Bill Phillips:

February 24, 1986

Being interviewed by ignorant reporters can be awful. The other day one of these idiots asked me, "How much does an advertising campaign cost in the USA?"

For once, I was speechless.

D.O.

(((

After David turned over his Chairmanship to Jack Elliott in 1975, he served the company as Creative Head, Worldwide, for a number of years. The following is from a memo he sent, in that capacity, to all heads of offices and creative heads:

July 18, 1977

Confusion?

I am told that some of you are confused by what you perceive as a change in my creative philosophy.

For many years you heard me inveigh against "entertainment" in TV commercials and "cleverness" in print advertising. When the advertising world went on a "creative" binge in the late 1960's, I denounced award winners as lunatics. Then I started the David Ogilvy Award – for the campaign which produced the biggest increase in *sales*.

You got the word.

Then, two years ago, you began to receive memos from me, complaining that too much of our output was stodgy and dull. Sometimes I circulated commercials and advertisements which I admired, but which appeared to violate my own principles.

Had I gone mad?

My original Magic Lantern started with the assertion that *Positioning* and *Promise* were more than half the battle. You accepted that, and proceeded accordingly.

But another slide in my dear old Lantern states that "unless your advertising contains a *Big Idea* it will pass like a ship in the night." Very few of you seem to have paid attention to that.

Three years ago I woke up to the fact that the majority of our campaigns, while impeccable as to positioning and promise, contained no big idea. They were too dull to penetrate the filter which consumers erect to protect themselves against the daily deluge of advertising. Too dull to be remembered. Too dull to build a brand image. Too dull to *sell*. ("You cannot *bore* people into buying your product.")

In short, we were still *sound*, but we were no longer *brilliant*. Neither soundness nor brilliance is any good by itself; each requires the other ...

So the time had come to give the pendulum a push in the other direction. If that push has puzzled you, caught you on the wrong foot and confused you, I can only quote Ralph Waldo Emerson:

"A foolish consistency is the hobgoblin of little minds ... Speak what you think today in words as hard as cannonballs, and tomorrow speak what tomorrow thinks in hard words again, though it contradict everything you said today."

I want all our offices to create campaigns which are second to none in positioning, promise – and brilliant ideas …

D.O.

A memo to the "syndicate heads" in New York:

May 7, 1970

TENURE

Most of the fashionable hotspots in the creative departments of other agencies are nomads, birds-of-passage.

It is not unusual for them to have worked at six agencies before they are thirty-two. What a turbulent, unsettling, dangerous way to live.

I have no stomach for recruiting these unprincipled adventurers.

By contrast, six of our seven Syndicate Heads have been at Ogilvy & Mather for an average of ten years. All the way from Reva's eighteen years to the eight years of such promising new arrivals as Gene, Bill and Tony.

I hope that these long tenures are good for the individuals. I *know* they are good for the agency.

Long may that last.

NOTE FROM D. O.

April 13, 1984

BILL PHILLIPS

Constitutional Monarchy

Walter Bagehot (pronounced bajjert),
the great English historian, wrote
that a constitutional monarch has
"the right to be consulted, the
right to encourage, the right to
warn."

Thank you for according me those
rights so generously.

From a memo commenting on the qualities of a 35-year-old creative director:

... He is still immature in some ways. For example, his "style" when presenting campaigns to clients is curiously boyish. This discomforts me – I prefer a posture of confident authority. But I have observed that many clients like his diffidence and humility. They seem to find it engaging and disarming.

His office is a pigsty. It does not *look* like the office of a top-management boss, and this can be a problem in a world which is impressed by appearances. Also, an untidy office suggests an untidy mind. I have to keep reminding myself that some very able men are untidy, and that some very stupid men are tidy ...

He administers his department rather loosely. But I doubt whether a rigid and orderly administration would fit a creative department. Some measure of informality and kaleidoscopic assignments are probably a good thing here ...

To the Management Supervisor on KLM:

March 3, 1969

I have always believed that tourists want fine weather on their vacations. Sunshine – not clouds.

The great tourist movements are towards the sun – from north to south. Hence the popularity of Florida, the Caribbean, the Mediterranean.

For years I have tried to get *sunny* photographs of Puerto Rico and Britain.

Now you are featuring photographs of Holland in fog and cloud. You must have a good reason for doing this. *What is it?*

D.O.

❨ ❨ ❨

A memo to creative heads:

April 17, 1980

A few weeks ago, I asked you to send me the names of anybody on your staff who might qualify to become a Creative Director.

Twenty of you sent me a total of 49 names.

One of you sent me *six* names – his entire creative staff, I suspect; charitable fellow.

Eleven of you told me that you have *nobody* who could qualify to become a Creative Director. You have problems. Something wrong with your hiring methods?

Ten of you have not answered. Bastards.

D.O.

A letter to David's 18-year-old great nephew in England:

June 6, 1984

Dear Harry,

You ask me whether you should spend the next three years at university, or get a job. I will give you three different answers. Take your pick.

Answer A. You are ambitious. Your sights are set on going to the top, in business or government. Today's big corporations cannot be managed by uneducated amateurs. In these high-tech times, they need top bananas who have doctorates in chemistry, physics, engineering, geology, etc.

Even the middle managers are at a disadvantage unless they boast a university degree and an MBA. In the United States, 18 percent of the population has a degree, in Britain, only 7 percent. Eight percent of Americans have graduate degrees, compared with 1 percent of Brits. That more than anything else is why American management outperforms British management.

Same thing in government. When I was your age, we had the best civil service in the world. Today, the French civil servants are better than ours because they are educated for the job in the postgraduate Ecole Nationale d'Administration, while ours go straight from Balliol to Whitehall. The French pros outperform the British amateurs.

Anyway, you are *too young* to decide what you want

to do for the rest of your life. If you spend the next few years at university, you will get to know the world – and yourself – before the time comes to choose your career.

Answer B. Stop frittering away your time in academia. Stop subjecting yourself to the tedium of textbooks and classrooms. Stop cramming for exams before you acquire an incurable hatred for reading.

Escape from the sterile influences of dons, who are nothing more than pickled undergraduates.

The lack of a college degree will only be a slight handicap in your career. In Britain, you can still get to the top without a degree. What industry and government need at the top is not technocrats but *leaders*. The character traits which make people scholars in their youth are not the traits which make them leaders in later life.

You put up with education for 12 boring years. Enough is enough.

Answer C. Don't judge the value of higher education in terms of careermanship. Judge it for what it is – a priceless opportunity to furnish your mind and enrich the qualify of your life. My father was a failure in business, but he read Horace in the loo until he died, poor but happy.

If you enjoy being a scholar, and like the company of scholars, go to a university. Who knows, you may end your days as a Regius Professor. And bear in mind that British universities are still the best in the world – at the undergraduate level. Lucky you. Winning a Nobel

Prize is more satisfying than being elected Chairman of some large corporation or becoming a Permanent Undersecretary in Whitehall.

You have a first-class mind. Stretch it. If you have the opportunity to go to a university, don't pass it up. You would never forgive yourself.

Tons of love,

David

From a memo to the Board, undated:

Not long ago, I overheard a conversation between two men sitting beside me in an airplane. It went like this:

"What business you in?"

  "I'm an account executive in an ad agency."

"Accountant?"

  "No."

"You write ads?"

  "No."

"Who writes the ads?"

  "Copywriters."

"That must be a fun job."

  "It's not that easy. We do a lot of research."

"<u>You</u> do the research?"

 "No, we have research people to do that."

"You sell the ads to the clients?"

 "No, the copywriters do that."

"Do you bring in new clients?"

 "That's not my job."

"Forgive me, but what <u>is</u> your job?"

 "I'm a marketing man."

"You do marketing for the clients?"

 "No, they do it themselves."

"Are you in Management?"

 "<u>No</u>, <u>but I soon will be</u>."

℞ ℞ ℞

From a memo to the Directors of Ogilvy & Mather preceding the arrival in their hands of his new book, "Ogilvy on Advertising", which none of them had yet seen:

July 25, 1983

(1) You will notice that I exaggerate my role in the agency today. I figured that few people would take me seriously if I came across as a man living in the past.

(2) I hope you will also notice repeated references to my *partners*. This is a change from the unrelieved

egotism of *Confessions*, and conveys the impression that Ogilvy & Mather is a large group of able people.

(3) The book includes many examples of good work by other agencies. I have never done this before. It is calculated to dilute the impression that the book is nothing more than a new business presentation for Ogilvy & Mather.

(4) Another departure: I admit several mistakes.

(5) You may feel that the book errs on the side of being anti-creative and pro-cash-register, and that this will damage our reputation. I have two excuses:

A) I wrote what I really believe. My last will and testament.

B) I think that more new business prospects will be attracted by the cash-register stuff than will be repelled by my attacks on pseudo-creativity.

David Ogilvy

•

An Australian journalist, compiling a book on lengthy careers, asked David how he has "lasted so long." Here are excerpts from his reply, sent to Australia in April 1986.

David Ogilvy's Marathon Innings

I am Scottish. When I was thirty-eight, I went to New York and started an advertising agency. It was an instant success and is now one of the biggest in the world, with 9,000 employees in 41 countries.

Now seventy-five, I am no longer Chairman of Ogilvy & Mather, but am still a Director and a member of the Executive Committee.

In the early days I could not afford to hire outstanding professionals, so I did almost everything myself ...

As my company's income grew, I was able to hire some able partners, but it remained a one-man band. I continued to monopolize all the power and all the publicity. If I had been hit by a taxi, Ogilvy & Mather would have gone up in smoke.

So I turned over a new leaf. I stopped seeing clients. Stepped out of the limelight. Stopped creating campaigns. Gave up day-to-day management. And started taking vacations – bicycling in France and vegetating on my farm in Pennsylvania.

This self-abnegation was difficult for me, but it worked. My partners blossomed, and the agency continued to grow – faster.

I have done my best to avoid getting in the hair of my successors. I take no part in line management ...

My successors and I have seen eye-to-eye on most issues. We have lived with the same corporate culture for 25 years.

I travel a lot, visiting Ogilvy & Mather offices in various countries – particularly those I can reach by train and ship; I am frightened of flying. Increasingly I am communicating by videocassette; tapes have more import than memoranda.

My marathon innings have been due, more than anything else, to four things:

1. I have outlived all my competitors.

2. My obsessive interest in advertising has not dimmed.

3. My younger partners have tolerated my presence in their midst.

4. I had the wisdom to give them a free run. As a result, Ogilvy & Mather has outgrown its founder.

HOBBIES

I cannot play golf, tennis or bridge. Only croquet. I cannot, alas, ski or sail. I still ride a bicycle.

I spend several hours a day working with my gardeners, and several hours at my desk.

And I read a great deal, mostly biography.

❰ ❰ ❰

A letter in response to a query from Ray Calt, an executive at another advertising agency:

April 19, 1955

Dear Mr. Calt:

On March 22nd you wrote to me asking for some notes on my work habits as a copywriter. They are appalling, as you are about to see:

1. I have never written an advertisement in the

office. Too many interruptions. I do all my writing at home.

2. I spend a long time studying the precedents. I look at every advertisement which has appeared for competing products during the past 20 years.

3. I am helpless without research material – and the more "motivational" the better.

4. I write out a definition of the problem and a statement of the purpose which I wish the campaign to achieve. Then I go no further until that statement and its principles have been accepted by the client.

5. Before actually writing the copy, I write down every conceivable fact and selling idea. Then I get them organized and relate them to research and the copy platform.

6. Then I write the headline. As a matter of fact I try to write 20 alternative headlines for every advertisement. And I never select the final headline without asking the opinions of other people in the agency. In some cases I seek the help of the research department and get them to do a split-run on a battery of headlines.

7. At this point I can no longer postpone doing the actual copy. So I go home and sit down at my desk. I find myself entirely without ideas.

   I get bad-tempered. If my wife comes into the room I growl at her. (This has gotten worse since I gave up smoking.)

8. I am terrified of producing a lousy advertisement. This causes me to throw away the first 20 attempts.

9. If all else fails, I drink half a bottle of rum and play a Handel oratorio on the gramophone. This generally produces an uncontrollable gush of copy.

10. Next morning I get up early and edit the gush.

11. Then I take the train to New York and my secretary types a draft. (I cannot type, which is very inconvenient.)

12. I am a lousy copywriter, but I am a good editor. So I go to work editing my own draft. After four or five editings, it looks good enough to show to the client. If the client *changes* the copy, I get angry – because I took a lot of trouble writing it, and what I wrote I wrote *on purpose*.

Altogether it is a slow and laborious business. I understand that some copywriters have much greater facility.

Yours sincerely,

D.O.

Rare photograph: Quite possibly a first attempt at typing.

Lists

Lists

David is fond of lists. Here are a few, the first from a talk to the staff:

The qualifications I look for in our leaders are these:

1. High standards of personal ethics.

2. *Big* people, without prettiness.

3. Guts under pressure, resilience in defeat.

4. Brilliant brains – not safe plodders.

5. A capacity for hard work and midnight oil.

6. Charisma – charm and persuasiveness.

7. A streak of unorthodoxy – creative innovators.

8. The courage to make tough decisions.

9. Inspiring enthusiasts – with thrust and gusto.

10. A sense of humor.

MIXED MARRIAGE

Although he admits to no prejudices regarding race, religion, etc. – and has never displayed any in his management practices – David is well aware of who's what.

One September day, shortly after a Jewish copywriter had married a Catholic copywriter, he came bounding down the hall and greeted the husband with "*Happy Saint Rosh Hashanah!*"

An account manager wrote to David wondering what he considered his worst shortcomings. The reply:

1. I am intolerant of mediocrity – and laziness.

2. I fritter away too much time on things which aren't important.

3. Like everyone of my age, I talk too much about the past.

4. I have always funked firing people who needed to be fired.

5. I am afraid of flying and go to ridiculous lengths to avoid it.

6. When I was Creative Head in New York, I wrote too much of the advertising myself.

7. I know nothing about finance.

8. I change my mind – about advertising and about people.

9. I am candid to the point of indiscretion.

10. I see too many sides to every argument.

11. I am over-impressed by physical beauty.

12. I have a low threshold of boredom.

2   2   2

To heads of U.S. offices, preceding a swing around the country:

February 2, 1981

MY VISIT

I have already sent you my schedule. Now Bill Phillips has suggested that I should give you "some idea of the things you would like to do in each city."

In principle, I place myself in your hands. However:

(1) The fewer speeches the better. I have to make big ones to an American Express meeting in Florida this month, and to the 4A's in April. I don't have much left to say, and writing speeches takes me forever.

(2) Maybe you could invite some people (staff and clients) to see my film *The View From Touffou*. To be followed by questions?

(3) I hate cocktail parties.

(4) I would like to visit with your best Creative people.

(5) I would like to meet major clients – *but only if I know*

something about their business. Which is not the case, for example, with Mattel.

(6) I get tired after 11 PM and go to bed.

(7) Please give me a little time-off to visit friends.

(8) Please don't meet me at the railroad station, and please don't see me off. I *hate* that. Let me arrive and depart *on my own.*

(9) Don't put me in a *suite* at the hotel. A *bedroom* is what I like.

(10) Please give me an office, however small. And a copy of *The New York Times* every day.

(11) I hate drinking in bars, and have to start eating the moment I sit down in restaurants. Waiting for food puts me in a foul mood.

D.O.

❖   ❖   ❖

A memo to the creative directors of Ogilvy & Mather offices worldwide:

July 1, 1979

ARE YOU THE GREATEST?

1. Are you creating the most remarkable advertising in your country?

2. Is this generally recognized, inside and outside your agency?

3. Can you show new-business prospects at least four campaigns which *electrify* them?

4. Have you stopped *overloading* commercials?

5. Have you stopped *singing* the sales pitch?

6. Do all your commercials start with a *visual grabber*?

7. Have you stopped using cartoon commercials when selling to adults?

8. Do you show at least six Magic Lanterns to everyone who joins your staff?

9. If they don't understand English, have you had all the Lanterns translated into their language?

10. Do you repeat the brand name several times in every commercial?

11. Have you stopped using celebrity testimonials in television commercials?

12. Have you got a list of red-hot creative people in other agencies, ready for the day when you can afford to hire them?

13. Do all your campaigns execute an agreed *positioning*?

14. Do they *promise a benefit* – which has been tested?

15. Do you always *super* the promise at least twice in every commercial?

16. Have you had at least three Big Ideas in the last six months?

17. Do you always *make the product the hero*?

18. Are you going to win more creative awards than any other agency this year?

19. Do you use problem-solution, humor, relevant characters, slice-of-life?

20. Do you eschew life-style commercials?

21. Do your people gladly work nights and weekends?

22. Are you good at injecting *news* into your campaign?

23. Do you always show the product in use?

24. Does your house reel include some commercials with irresistible *charm*?

25. Do you always show the package at the end?

26. Have you stopped using visual clichés – like sunsets and happy families at the dinner table? Do you use lots of *visual surprises*?

27. Do the illustrations in your print advertisements contain *story appeal*?

28. Are you phasing out *addy* layouts and moving to *editorial* layouts?

29. Do you sometimes use *visualized contrast*?

30. Do all your headlines contain the brand name – and the promise?

31. Are all your illustrations photographs?

32. Have you stopped setting copy ragged left and right?

33. Have you stopped using more than forty characters in a line of copy?

34. Have you stopped setting copy smaller than 10 point and bigger than 12 point?

35. Do you always paste advertisements into magazines or newspapers before you OK them?

36. Have you stopped setting body copy in sans-serif?

37. Have you stopped beating your wife?

If you can answer YES to all these questions, you are the greatest Creative Director on the face of the earth.

D.O.

∾ ∾ ∾

A memo drafted for the management to circulate as it saw fit:

September 7, 1982

HOW TO WRITE

If everybody in our company took an exam in writing, the highest marks would go to the 14 Directors.

The better you write, the higher you go in Ogilvy & Mather. People who *think* well, *write* well.

Woolly minded people write woolly memos, woolly letters and woolly speeches.

Good writing is not a natural gift. You have to *learn* to write well. Here are 10 hints:

(1) Read the Roman-Raphaelson book on writing.* Read it three times.

(2) Write the way you talk. Naturally.

(3) Use short words, short sentences and short paragraphs.

(4) Never use jargon words like *reconceptualize, demassification, attitudinally, judgmentally*. They are hallmarks of a pretentious ass.

(5) Never write more than two pages on any subject.

(6) Check your quotations.

(7) Never send a letter or a memo on the day you write it. Read it aloud the next morning – and then edit it.

(8) If it is something important, get a colleague to improve it.

(9) Before you send your letter or your memo, make sure it is crystal clear what you want the recipient to do.

(10) If you want ACTION, *don't write*. Go and *tell* the guy what you want.

David

---

*Writing That Works, Harper & Row, 1981.

Another note to the Board:

January 24, 1983

INDIA

I seem to be big in India. The Sunday Magazine recently published photographs of 54 men and women who made news in 1982. Eleven of them were not Indians:

Andropov

Brezhnev

David Ogilvy

Mitterand

Princess Diana

Pope John Paul II

Lech Walesa

Ayatolla Khomeini

Yasser Arafat

Jimmy Connors

Menachem Begin

Wanted by
Ogilvy & Mather International
Trumpeter Swans

In my experience, there are five kinds of Creative Director:

1. Sound on strategy, dull on execution.

2. Good managers who don't make waves... and don't produce brilliant campaigns either.

3. Duds.

4. The genius who is a lousy leader.

5. TRUMPETER SWANS who combine personal genius with inspiring leadership.

We have an opening for one of these rare birds in one of our offices overseas.

Write in inviolable secrecy to me, David Ogilvy, Touffou, 86300 Bonnes, France.

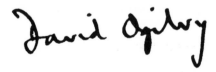

Note to Trumpeter Swans:
David Ogilvy no longer handles job applications.
Write to Ogilvy & Mather in your country.

This list, sent to the Board, was later converted into the "help wanted"
advertisement overleaf:

May 23, 1981

Five Kinds of Creative Heads

(1) Those whose personal talent amounts to genius;
they don't always make the best managers.

(2) Good managers who get the work out – punctual
and competent. They don't make waves, but they
don't make hot agencies either.

(3) Help on strategy. Useful on some accounts. Apt to
be dull.

(4) Trumpeter Swans. *Very* rare birds. They combine
personal genius with inspiring leadership.

(5) Duds.

D.O.

From Flagbearer, *the New York office's staff newsletter:*

November 19, 1976

Somebody recently asked me for a list of the most
useful books on advertising – the books that all our
people should read. Here is what I sent her:

1. *Scientific Advertising* by Claude Hopkins;
Foreword by David Ogilvy. Crown
Publishers.

2. *Tested Advertising Methods* by John Caples; Foreword by David Ogilvy. Prentice-Hall.

3. *Confessions of an Advertising Man* by David Ogilvy. Atheneum Publishers.

4. *How to Advertise* by Kenneth Roman and Jane Maas; Foreword by David Ogilvy. St Martin's Press.

5. *Reality in Advertising* by Rosser Reeves. Alfred Knopf.

6. *The Art of Writing Advertising* by Bernbach, Burnett, Gribbin, Ogilvy & Reeves. Advertising Publications, Inc., Chicago.

7. *The 100 Best Advertisements* by Julian Watkins. Dover Publications.

A note to the Board of Directors:

October 21, 1982

"The Pope of Modern Advertising"

The current issue of Jean-Louis Servan-Schreiber's magazine, EXPANSION, is devoted to the Industrial Revolution and lists thirty men who have contributed to it. They include:

Thomas Edison

Albert Einstein

John Maynard Keynes

Alfred Krupp

Lenin

Karl Marx

David Ogilvy – "the Pope of modern advertising"

Louis Pasteur

James de Rothschild

Adam Smith

Thomas J. Watson Sr.

Will the College of Cardinals please come to order?

D.O.

In "Raise Your Sights" – a list of 97 tips for copywriters, art directors, and TV producers – this was saved for last:

97. Whenever you write a commercial, bear in mind that it is likely to be seen by your children, your wife – and your conscience.

Addressing annual staff meeting in New York in 1979.

Speeches and Papers

Speeches and Papers

The opening section of a talk delivered in 1949, the year after the agency opened, by David Ogilvy, Vice President and Research Director of Hewitt, Ogilvy, Benson & Mather.

These early remarks, on "Research and its Effect on the Visual Phases of Advertising," were addressed to the Art Directors Forum in New York. They sound a theme often revisited over the decades.

Here are two ads for the same product. They are the same size. They cost the same. But one reached 31 times as many prospects as the other.

What would you think if the space-buyer in your agency could buy 31 times as much circulation per dollar as other space-buyers?

You would think he was the most important man in the agency business. That is exactly the position you art directors are in.

It is within your power to reach 31 times as many readers per dollar as other art directors.

That is a big difference.

Your space-buyer buys gross circulation, your copy-writer gives you the selling story, and *your* job is to deliver the largest possible net circulation for that story ...

Your job, as I see it, is to take the selling appeal you are given, and then go to work and deliver the maximum audience. I mean audience of *prospects*.

That is where research can help art directors. It can give you some indication as to the type of visual treatment which will deliver the most *prospects per dollar* ...

~ ~ ~

From a speech at the Annual Advertising Awards dinner, announcing the winner of the Career Award for Distinguished Personal Services to Advertising for 1953:

January 21, 1954

The Juries which select the winners of this award have an extremely difficult job.

This year, for example, we had *almost a hundred* nominations placed before us ...

So we got to studying the list of men who had won the award in the past.

We noticed that it included

great publishers,

great advertising managers,

distinguished officers of associations,

men who have worked for great causes,
above and beyond the call of duty,

and heads of great agencies.

We thought it was curious that the Award had been given so seldom – if ever – for *creative* services.

After all, it is the creative man who makes the product upon which the whole structure of our business depends.

Unless the creative man produces *great advertisements*, the rest of us might as well pack up and go home.

So we decided, in principle, to give the Gold Medal Award to a great creative man.

We hoped that, by so doing, we would sound a trumpet call to the copywriters and art directors who work day after day at their typewriters and their drawing boards.

Generally speaking, you don't hear much about these people. Most of them are more or less unsung – if not totally invisible and anonymous.

It is not surprising that these creative people sometimes get the idea that nobody thinks they matter very much.

By giving the Gold Medal to one of these creative men, the Jury goes on record as believing that nobody in all advertising matters more than the copywriter and the art director …*

---

* *Editor*'s *note*: The award went to Roy Whittier, a distinguished copywriter at Young & Rubicam.

From "What the Creative Man Can Do to Increase Public Acceptance of Advertising," a speech to the Association of National Advertisers, March 1954:

I have only one complaint to make about our session here this morning. It is this: all the speakers are on the same side of the fence. We are all against sin.

Next year I would like to see A.N.A. stage a great *debate*, with one of our more notorious malefactors here to defend his position. One of the unrepentant weasel merchants.

We might couple him up to a lie detector and then invite him to read some of his own copy out loud.

* * * * *

I have been asked to talk to you about "the growing lack of public confidence in advertising." First let me say this: I'm far from sure in my own mind that lack of public confidence *is* growing.

It would be a hard thing to prove. After all, Dr. Gallup wasn't around to measure public confidence in the bad old days before our reform movement got started.

But of one thing I am very sure. There is a growing uneasiness *within our own ranks*. Most of the thoughtful men and women I know in the agency field, and particularly the younger generation, are becoming increasingly introspective about their profession – and the part it plays in the body economic …

TRUTH AND WEASELS

Now I come to *truth* in advertising.

Here again, I don't know the precise state of public opinion. Personally, I think that actual truth has become more or less a dead issue. Most advertising nowadays is a great deal more truthful than the public realizes.

Our problem is to make the public believe the true things we say. It's no use telling the truth if people don't believe you. So, how can we copywriters make our ads more believable?

Well, we can start by turning our backs on the *weasel*. The kind of weasels which still disgrace so much advertising for toothpaste, cigarettes, detergents and low-calorie-beer. The kind of weasels that depreciate the whole currency of copy.

Verbal weasels and *typographical* weasels. Most of us on the creative side are connoisseurs of the weasel. Far more than the public, we comprehend the villainies of the weasel merchants ...

Let's take our tongues out of our cheeks. Let's try and write like human beings.

We hope that you people, our clients, will encourage us in this, because most of us are very sensitive to what our clients are thinking.

TRY THIS EXPERIMENT

If any of you gentlemen have any private qualms about the continued presence of weasels in your own advertising, I want to suggest that you try a novel experiment.

When you get back to your office on Monday morning, send for your agency people and address them in these terms:

> "Our production people are very proud of their product. They think it's such a damn good product that you ought to be able to advertise it without weaseling.

> "Our stockholders include a lot of widows and orphans. Sure, they need profits and dividends. But they don't want you to cheat in pursuit of their dividends.

> "So please take another look at the advertising we have scheduled for 1954. Ask yourself if you would feel any compunction about exposing *your own* children to it.

> "Ask yourself if any of it could possibly fan the flames of public resentment against advertising.

> "Ask yourself if any of it could possibly damage our company's reputation *in the long run*.

> "Ask finally, ask yourself if any of it is in conflict with your own private standards of morality

and good taste. As your clients, we have no desire to increase the load of guilt you carry through life."

But one word of warning. This can be an extremely *dangerous* experiment. If you decide to try it, I advise you to make it crystal clear to your agency that you aren't looking for soft, gutless advertising. And that you aren't looking for mere entertainment.

Explain that you still want advertising with selling teeth in it. *Honest* teeth, but *biting* teeth.

The effect on your agency may well be electrifying. I can imagine nothing better calculated to stimulate creative people to produce great advertising for you ...

* * * * *

Every time you run an advertisement that is genuinely *creative* and *interesting*, you not only benefit your own company, but all your fellow advertisers.

If we in the agency business can create enough interesting campaigns, we can get consumers to drop their resistance.

Don't let's be dull bores. We can't save souls in an empty church.

HELP FOR A COMPETITOR

Someone in the Sydney office of another agency sent David a telex asking him to answer a question, as fodder for a speech.

The question: *"What single step would most enhance our reputation for creativity?"*

The telexed reply: *"Change the name of your agency to Ogilvy."*

From "The Image and the Brand – a New Approach to Creative Operations," a talk to the American Association of Advertising Agencies in Chicago, October 1955:

When I was invited to speak at luncheon here today, Fred Gamble suggested that I should build my talk around a Creative Credo which I had recently circulated to some of my friends. That sounded delightfully easy. So I agreed.

But the following week Sid Bernstein got hold of a copy of my Credo and printed it in *Advertising Age*. That put the kibosh on my talk.

So now I have decided to take just one plank out of my Credo, and preach you a short sermon on that one text. It happens to be the first plank, and this is what it says:

> *"Every advertisement is part of the long-term investment in the personality of the brand."*

I didn't make that up. I borrowed it, from an article by Burleigh Gardner and Sidney Levy in the March issue of the Harvard Business Review. It is exactly the position we take at Ogilvy, Benson & Mather today.

We hold that every advertisement must be considered as a contribution to the complex symbol which is the brand image – as part of the long-term investment in the reputation of the brand.

I must confess that I have changed my mind on this subject. When I first arrived in this country eighteen years ago, I bought the wicked old Chicago philosophy, as practiced by Claude Hopkins.

I used to deride advertising men who talked about *long-term effect*. I used to accuse them of *hiding behind* long-term effect. I used to say that they used long-term effect as an alibi – to conceal their inability to make any single advertisement profitable. In those intolerant days I believed that every advertisement must stand on its own two feet and sell goods at a profit on the cost of the space …

Today, I have come to believe, with Gardner and Levy, that every advertisement must be considered as a contribution to the complex symbol which is the brand image. And I find that if you take that long-term approach, a great many of the day-to-day creative questions answer themselves …

During the last six months we have seen a remarkable demonstration of image building for a new brand. I refer to Marlboro Cigarettes. Leo Burnett and his associates used *judgment* to decide what kind of image to create for the Marlboro image – before they started to create the advertising.

And incidentally they took a risk which few advertisers would take. They seem to have decided that Marlboro should have an exclusively *male* personality. What a brave decision.*

I find that most manufacturers are reluctant to accept any such limitation on the image and personality of their brands. They want to be all things to all people. They want their brand to be a male brand *and* a female brand. An upper-crust brand *and* a plebeian brand.

And in their greed they almost always end up with a brand which has no personality of any kind – a wishy-washy *neuter* brand. No capon ever rules the roost – and neuter brands get no place in today's market …

What would you think of a politician who changed his public personality every year? Have you noticed that Winston Churchill has been careful to wear the same ties and the same hats for fifty years – so as not to confuse us?

Think of all the forces that work to *change* the personality and image of the brand from season to season. The advertising managers come and go. The copywriters, the art directors, and the account executives come and go. Even the agencies come and go.

What guts it takes, what obstinate determination, to stick to one coherent creative policy, year after year, in the face of all the pressures to "come up with something new" every six months …

**Editor's note*: This campaign, then just six months old, is still running 32 years later.

APPLICANT WITH SEEING-EYE DOG

In the early 1960s, Ogilvy & Mather still had separate copy and art departments. Late one winter afternoon Cliff Field, who was in charge of copy for the massive new Shell account, interviewed a blind man.

It was dark and snowing hard, so after the interview Cliff escorted the applicant to the street to try to find him a taxi.

David came to look for him, asked somebody where he was, and was told: "I don't quite know, Sir. The last I saw of him he was getting on the elevator in his shirt sleeves, with a blind man and his seeing-eye dog."

David smote his forehead: *"My God! Clifford's hiring an art director!"*

Among those who like to debate the merits of "rational" vs. "emotional" advertising, David somehow got labeled an all-out champion of reason. The label has stuck, but doesn't bear scrutiny. The following excerpt, from a 1957 talk in England to the Advertising Association Conference, sounds a note played often, both in earlier and later years:

I am astonished to find how many manufacturers, on both sides of the Atlantic, still believe that women can be persuaded by *logic* and *argument* to buy one brand in preference to another – even when the two brands are technically identical.

The greater the similarity between products, the less part reason plays in brand selection.

There really isn't any significant difference between the various brands of whiskey, or the various cigarettes, or the various brands of beer. They are all about the same. And so are the cake mixes and the detergents, and the margarines, and even the motor cars.

The manufacturer who dedicates his advertising to building the most favourable *image*, the most sharply defined *personality*, is the one who will get the largest share of the market at the highest profit – in the long run.

In our agency we take a long view of our creative responsibilities. We plan ten years ahead, on the assumption that our clients are not out for a fast buck, but intend to stay in business forever.

We try to create sharply defined personalities for our brands. And we *stick* to those personalities, year after year.

* * *

From "The New Business Policies of Ogilvy, Benson & Mather," a paper written in 1960 for the guidance of the management:

We have exercised care in selecting our clients. That is why our roster is such a remarkable one.

We seek clients who manufacture a product which we can be proud to advertise – a product which we can recommend without reservation to our own families.

We see clients whose basic attitudes to business are about the same as ours. The agency-client relationship is an intimate one, and it only works well when there is a strong ingredient of mutual respect on both sides.

We seek accounts on which we can make a profit. Ten years' experience with cost accounting has taught us which kind of accounts are likely to be unprofitable; we avoid them.

We want Ogilvy & Mather to be the *best* agency. That is one reason why we exercise so much restraint in controlling the speed of our expansion. We must avoid growing so rapidly that our standards of service would have to be diluted.

∽ ∽ ∽

From a 1960 statement to the Senate Committee on Interstate and Foreign Commerce, advocating an advertising campaign to attract European tourists to the United States:

One word of warning. When the time comes for the new Office of International Travel & Tourism to advertise in foreign countries, I suggest that those concerned should be careful not to put anything into their advertisements which could hurt the image of the United States. Indeed, they should try to create advertising which will *improve* that image ...

To run a campaign of this kind in fourteen European countries would cost about $1,362,000 a year for space – say $2,000,000 by the time you have paid for the photographs and the engravings, and the collateral promotion. That's about the cost of one fighter aircraft.

In his decades as the boss, David liked to speak candidly to the staff at Christmas, summing up the year's performance, setting goals for the future, and reaffirming standards. From his talk in 1960:

Before I turn to the future, I would like to preach my perennial sermon on the subject of *behaviour*. I want the newcomers to know what kind of behaviour we admire, and what kind of behaviour we deplore:

1. First, we admire people who *work hard*. We dislike passengers who don't pull their weight in the boat.

2. We admire people with first-class brains, because you cannot run a great advertising agency without brainy people.

3. We admire people who *avoid politics* – office politics, I mean.

4. We despise toadies who suck up to their bosses; they are generally the same people who bully their subordinates.

5. We admire the great professionals, the craftsmen who do their jobs with superlative excellence. We notice that these people always respect the professional expertise of their colleagues in other departments.

6. We admire people who hire subordinates who are good enough to succeed them. We pity people who are so insecure that they feel compelled to hire inferior specimens as their subordinates.

7. We admire people who build up and develop their subordinates, because this is the only way we can promote from within the ranks. We detest having to go outside to fill important jobs, and I look forward to the day when that will never be necessary.

8. We admire people who practice delegation. The more you delegate, the more responsibility will be loaded upon you.

9. We admire kindly people with gentle manners who treat other people as human beings – particularly the people who sell things to us. We abhor *quarrelsome* people. We abhor people who wage paper welfare. We abhor buck passers, and people who don't tell the truth.

10. We admire well-organized people who keep their offices shipshape, and deliver their work on time.

11. We admire people who are good citizens in their communities – people who work for their local hospitals, their church, the PTA, the Community Chest and so on.

* * *

In his talk to the staff at Christmas in 1962, David quoted responses to an internal survey on the strengths and weaknesses of the Agency. This excerpt starts about halfway through the talk.

Those are the main points on the *positive* side – esprit de corps, hard work, high standards of professional performance, guts in telling our clients the truth, a clearly defined point of view, and better advertising campaigns.

So far, so good. But now we come to the *bad* part.

PROBLEMS OF SIZE

One particularly thoughtful individual has this to say:

> "As we grow, it seems to me to be more difficult to maintain that great esprit de corps. I have had a feeling that some of our great vitality is waning, and that the agency has less of that zip, bustle and excitement that were so prominent during the first years."

… Here I want to address those of you who head up departments and account groups, and indeed everyone who is the boss of anyone else. I look to *you* to become our main sources of inspiration. Perhaps you will not mind if I offer you some advice on how to go about it:

A) Don't *overstaff* your departments. People enjoy life most when they have the most work to do.

B) Set exorbitant standards, and give your people hell when they don't live up to them. There is nothing so demoralizing as a boss who tolerates second-rate work.

C) When your people turn in an exceptional performance, make sure they know you admire them for it.

D) Don't let your people fall into a rut. Keep leading them along new paths, blazing new trails. Give them a sense of *adventurous pioneering*.

E) Do your best to *educate* your people, so that they can be promoted as rapidly as possible.

F) Delegate. Throw your people in over their heads. That is the only way to find out how good they are.

G) Seek *advice* from your subordinates, and listen more than you talk.

H) Above all, make sure that you are getting the most out of all your people. Men and women are happiest when they know that they are giving everything they've got.

RIGIDITY

Another criticism I have received is that we are *too rigid in applying our creative principles*:

"Here at Ogilvy, Benson & Mather campaigns are developed according to the disciplines you have established. There is a danger that these disciplines are interpreted too narrowly."

I make no apology for having established a set of creative principles, but I cannot believe that they represent the last word. I am hungry for younger creative people to come along and enlarge our philosophies.

Start where I leave off.

TOO MUCH PAPER

Another criticism I have received is that there is far too much *paper* around here:

> "One of the first differences I noticed on coming over was the volume of paper work. The amount of it is bad. But what it reflects is good. Much of the paper is the result of a lot of people thinking and having thoughts about a problem.

> "A case in point was the torrent that flowed while the 1963 Shell plan was being developed. A score of people were having thoughts. And they had the enthusiasm and the energy to *write them down*."

O.K., but I wish to heaven they wouldn't write them down at such exorbitant *length*. Really, the amount of paper we have to read nowadays is horrible. For Pete's sake write shorter memos. Don't argue with each other on paper. Don't send copies of trivial memos to 29 people ...

I would like you all to make a New Year's Resolution. Cut your wordage in *half*. This will make it possible for us to finish our homework before midnight.

* * * * *

Well, I have now reported the three negatives – the problem of inspiration in an agency which is no longer small; rigidity in applying our creative principles; and too much paper.

Adding it all up, the pros and cons, how does Ogilvy, Benson & Mather look to me? How does the OBM of 1962 compare with the agency I dreamed of in 1948?

To tell you the truth, it looks a million times better than I ever dreamed it could look. I just cannot *believe* what a good agency this has grown to be. *I am terribly proud, and terribly grateful.*

◆　◆　◆

From a talk to the National Industrial Conference Board, April 1961:

… There is no great trick to *doing* research. The problem is to get people to *use* it – particularly when the research reveals that you have been making mistakes.

We all have a tendency to use research as a drunkard uses a lamppost – for support, not for illumination.

Before Pearl Harbor, the United States Government succeeded in deciphering the telegrams which the Japanese Ambassador in Washington was sending back to Tokyo, reporting his conversations with Cordell Hull. Unfortunately, there was a failure to act on this intelligence.

Later on, the Navy was able to crack the Japanese Naval cipher. This time somebody acted on the intelligence. The happy result was the victory at Midway.

It's the same way in marketing. The problem is to find people with the guts to *act* on intelligence reports, particularly when they are unfavourable.

PECULIAR BEHAVIOR

David is often astonished by working habits that differ from his own. Once, discussing a copywriter at another agency whom he admired in some respects, he said:

> "Listen to this – every day at precisely five o'clock that man gets up from his desk, puts on his hat and his coat, and goes home."

Long pause to let it sink in. Then, leaning forward for emphasis: "Think of the extraordinary self-discipline that requires!"

In the modern corporation, who should have the responsibility for reading research reports and deciding what action should be taken? When I was a child I used to lie in bed early in the morning, debating with myself as to what servants I would employ when I grew up and got rich. Would I start by hiring a chef, a chauffeur, a gardener, a butler, or a masseur?

Nowadays, I lie in bed wondering who I would hire if I became a manufacturer. I am inclined to think that I would start with a research analyst – even before an advertising manager …

From a dinner talk to the St Andrew's Society, November 1962:

Mr. President, Mr. Consul-General, Lord Strathclyde, Sir Alexander Brackenridge, fellow members of the St Andrew's Society.

Today is the birthday of Sir Winston Churchill. I remember an incident which took place at the end of the Casablanca Conference.

It was the last morning, after the official business was finished. Sir Winston sent for his security officer. The old man had just finished breakfast and was lying in bed smoking a cigar. When the security officer entered the bedroom, Churchill looked up at him and said: "Codrington, I want to visit the *bazaars*."

Codrington said that he would have to consult his American colleagues, who were responsible for the security of both delegations. The Americans promptly vetoed the expedition as too dangerous. This placed poor Codrington in a ticklish position, because he knew from bitter experience that Churchill would not like being thwarted.

However, he was an ingenious fellow, so he said to the Prime Minister: "The Americans don't want you to go. German assassins have been parachuted around Casablanca, and there is no time for the Military Police to clear the streets where the bazaars are situated. The Americans think it would be most *dangerous* for you to go. Of course I have explained to them that you are indifferent to all considerations of personal danger. So I suppose that you may as well go.

"However, Sir, there is one thing I would like to point out. The bazaars are full of *disease*. If *you* were to catch one of these diseases, it wouldn't matter – you have the constitution of an ox. But I must remind you that your friend, Mr. Roosevelt, is extremely *delicate* and if he caught the disease from you, well, the consequences might be tragic."

Churchill winked, and said, "All right, Codrington, I won't visit the bazaars. However, I would like you to know that I was not planning to visit the bazaars for the particular purpose you seem to have in mind; and even if I had been, and had I had the misfortune to contract one of those loathsome diseases to which you are evidently referring, I can assure you that I would not have transmitted it to the President of the United States."

* * * * *

I would like to speak in praise of Scotland, my native country. Last time a member of my family tried this he got into terrible trouble.

My Ogilvy kinsman was talking to Oliver Goldsmith – and that repulsive old English bore Samuel Johnson. Here's how it went, according to Boswell:

> "Mr. Ogilvy was unlucky enough to choose for the topic of his conversation the praises of his native country. He began with saying that there was very rich land around Edinburgh. Goldsmith, who had studied physic there, contradicted this, with a sneering laugh.
>
> "Disconcerted a little by this, Mr. Ogilvy then took a new ground, where, I suppose, he thought himself

perfectly safe, for he observed that Scotland had a great many noble wild prospects."

It was at this point that Dr. Johnson delivered his famous snub to my unfortunate ancestor:

"Norway, too, has noble wild prospects; and Lapland is remarkable for prodigious, noble, wild prospects. But, Sir, let me tell you, the noblest prospect which a Scotchman ever sees is the highroad that leads him to England!"

I kicked the bottom out of my cradle the first time I heard that story. But I couldn't resist telling it again, because it shows the danger we Ogilvys run when we boast about Scotland.

* * *

From a speech to the Life Insurance Agency Management Association delivered in 1965 – some years before direct mail became a major factor in selling insurance:

... The time has come, I suggest, to test some revolutionary innovations.

Murray D. Lincoln is fond of saying that what every big organization needs is a "Vice-President in charge of revolution." Today I have elected myself as Vice-President in charge of *your* revolution.

Here, then, is a revolution for you to test. *Test direct mail.*

I suspect that your best prospect is your present policyholder. You know all about him – his name and address, his age, how many children he has, his occupation, his medical record, his wife's name, and so on. It is time you made some use of this gold mine of intelligence.

I believe that you can sell a lot of insurance, very cheaply, to your present policyholders by using direct mail – *good* direct mail ...

One insurance company I know spends sixty times as much on salesmen's commissions as it spends on selling by direct mail. Many companies spend *nothing* on selling by direct mail. Goodness knows why not. Maybe they just never got around to it.

I myself have life insurance policies with three companies. Not one of them has ever written me a letter suggesting that I buy *more* insurance from them. All they ever send me is premium notices.

Bloody fools ...

❦   ❦   ❦

From an ad-lib talk to the Direct Mail Advertising Association in Washington in October 1965, after Ogilvy & Mather's five-page letter for Mercedes-Benz had won the Gold Mail Box Award for the best direct mail campaign of 1964:

I have owned a few motor cars in my life ... I have never received a selling letter from one of the factories whose cars I drive suggesting that maybe the time had come for me to get a new one.

They simply don't do it.

I'm here to predict that in the next five years you

are going to see the advertising agencies – the good ones – grow up into Direct Mail. You are going to see Direct Mail emerge as a medium we agency people use, and use professionally.

    ℰ   *ℰ*   *ℰ*

From "Ten Bees in My Bonnet," a talk at a dinner at Colby College in June 1966. David was a Colby Trustee. Here are his introductory remarks, and five of his ten "bees":

What I am going to say does not in any way reflect the views of your Board of Trustees. I speak only for myself.

I am not an alumnus of Colby – or indeed of any other American college. I went to Oxford, 3,500 miles away. This places me at some disadvantage. If anyone wants to say that I don't know what I am talking about, I can only plead that my relative detachment helps me to see things through an objective eye.

What I know about Colby and other colleges derives from four sources:

First, from listening to the talk at meetings of the Colby Board of Trustees during the last four years.

Second, from reading a good deal about education in general, and other colleges in particular.

Third, from observing my son's experiences at the University of Virginia.

Fourth, from being married to a Barnard undergraduate.

I have come to some general conclusions, and this is my opportunity to ventilate them. They are more than conclusions – they are veritable *bees in my bonnet*.

1. First, I agree with Professor Nathan Glazer that "A very large part of what students and teachers do in the *best* colleges and universities is sheer waste."

I will now prove this.

Dr. Gallup tested a cross section of college graduates of all ages, all over the country. He found that 62 percent cannot identify Immanuel Kant.

Two thirds cannot translate the word *sister* into French *or* German *or* Spanish.

Less than half can name the Chief Justice of the Supreme Court. Only half know that elections for seats in the House of Representatives are held every two years.

One third have not read a single book of any kind during the last year.

If Dr. Gallup had confined his poll to *Colby* graduates, instead of interviewing a cross section of *all* college graduates, the results might have been somewhat more encouraging.

However, I am inclined to think that the present system of college education, even here at Colby, needs improvement …

HEADMASTER

When Dave McCall was Associate Copy Chief at Ogilvy, Benson & Mather, he had dinner with David and his teenage son, David Fairfield Ogilvy. Much of the talk centered on the prep school David's son was going to and how, if David were headmaster, he'd run things there.

After a while his son said, "Well *I* sure wouldn't want to go to any school where *you* were headmaster."

David's fatherly response: "That's a rather rude thing to say in present company. Mr. McCall *goes* to such a school."

---

* * * * *

3. I would like to see tenure abolished.

The tenure system is imposed on colleges by the American Association of University Professors – which is one of the most powerful trade unions I have ever encountered.

The pity is that the students don't have a trade union of their own, to protect them against the all-powerful professors' union.

The case for tenure revolves around the protection of teachers who advocate unorthodox theories. Such protection is, of course, very desirable indeed. But I believe that it is even more desirable to protect students from poor teachers …

Incidentally, it is preposterous that tenure should

be a *one-way* contract. If a professor cannot be sacked, he should also be unable to quit in search of richer pastures in another college ...

* * * * *

5. Next I come to *psychiatry*.

A lot of people still regard psychiatry as new-fangled nonsense – until their children drop out of college, or are sent to the Menninger Clinic with a serious breakdown.

There are now eleven psychiatrists on the medical staff at Harvard. How many at Colby? None – not one.

This is silly. A psychiatrist could do a great deal for students who get mixed-up – and a lot of students do, nowadays.

No Colby student should be flunked out until he has had a few sessions with a psychiatrist. This would save a lot of students – and it is our duty to save them, if we possibly can.

6. A college of limited resources cannot achieve the same degree of distinction in *all* its academic departments.

There is a hue and cry to add new departments at Colby. I would prefer to concentrate on increasing the excellence of some of our present departments; we have some excellent departments. I agree with the Oxford don who said, "The strength of a college can be measured by the number of subjects it *refuses* to teach."

7. I believe that one of the most useful things we can teach our students is to write lucid reports. If you are going to be a businessman, you won't get far unless you can write lucid reports – and very few college graduates can. If you are going to be a doctor, it will help if you can contribute lucid articles to medical journals. Knowledge is useless unless you know how to communicate it – in writing.

* * * * *

From a talk to the students at Fettes, David's school in Scotland, on Founder's Day, 1968:

My family's connection with Fettes goes back 111 years. In 1857 my Great Uncle Lord Inglis of Glencorse became a Trustee. Lord Normand used to say that it was in great measure due to my Uncle that Fettes takes the form it now bears.

Well, Uncle John may have been a great judge, *but apparently he could not read a will*.

Sir William Fettes left the residue of his estate "for the maintenance, education, and outfit of young people whose parents ... are unable to give suitable education to their *children*."

Sir William Fettes specified *children*. Now I ask you, fellow Fettesians, what right had my dear old Uncle to decide that Sir William meant only *boy* children?

... I wonder how many of you boys would like to see girls admitted to Fettes. Let us be democratic. Let us take a vote. Will those in favor of girls please raise their right hands?

The motion is carried, NEMINE CONTRADICENTE.

If the Governors continue to ignore the wishes of our Founder, I expect you boys will follow the example of your contemporaries at many great universities: *riot*.

• • •

I am deeply sorry for the present generation of Fettesians. You have to endure the horrors of A levels and O levels. The masters have to cram you full of facts, so that you can pass those odious examinations. This is like cramming corn down the throat of a goose to enlarge his liver. It may produce excellent pâté de foie gras, but it does the goose no permanent good.

The mission of a great school is not to cram you with facts so that you can regurgitate them a few weeks later at an exam. This gives many boys such a distaste for learning that they never read another book as long as they live. No, the mission is to inspire you with a taste for scholarship – a taste which will last you all your life. Dr. Potts inspired that taste in my father – he read Horace in the lavatory to his dying day.

It was not conventional crammers who inspired me at Fettes. It was eccentric scholars – Mr. Sellar, Mr. Pyatt, Mr. Newman and Dr. Havergal. God bless them!

Alas, I wasn't a great scholar. I was a duffer at games. I detested the philistines who ruled the roost. I was an irreconcilable rebel – a misfit. In short, I was a dud.

In the last edition of the Fettes register, Lord Normand – then Chairman of the Governors – wrote something remarkably candid:

"To be a dud in a large school where only classical learning counts in the form room, and only cricket and football outside it, is little better than living in a concentration camp."

•   •   •

My only claim to fame was that I was the first prefect who refused to take part in corporal punishment; I refused to do any beating.

… Last summer the Queen asked me what I did for a living. When I said ADVERTISING, you should have seen the expression on her beautiful face – a mixture of horror, incredulity, and amusement.

Far be it from me to argue with the Sovereign – or the Headmaster. I can only plead that QUIDVIS RECTE FACTUM, QUAMVIS HUMILE, PREACLARUM. "Whatever you do in life, however humble, is OK if you do it right."

I think that motto would apply to our Founder. Sir William Fettes was a grocer, but he did it right. So don't let's look down our noses at grocers – or even advertising men. Indeed, I dare to suggest that if Fettes produced more marketers and advertising men, Britain's balance of payments would not be in such miserable shape.

•   •   •

On Founder's Day four years ago, my old friend Lord Drumalbyn advised you to "avoid excess in all things." Mr. Ashcroft used to say the same thing – avoid excess in all things.

That is a recipe for dullness and mediocrity – in my humble opinion …

• • •

From a talk to executives of McKinsey & Company, February 1972:

When I was a boy, we used to sing a song:

> *"Who takes care of the caretaker's daughter*
>
> *When the caretaker's busy taking care?"*

I have always wondered who management consultants consult. Now I know. You consult *me*, that's who.

I cannot tell you what a charge I got when Marvin Bower invited me to come here today. My admiration for Marvin, and for McKinsey, amounts to hero-worship. My partners are sick to death of hearing me exhort them to conduct our business the way you guys conduct yours.

It occurs to me that McKinsey and Ogilvy & Mather have a few things in common:

> We are both service businesses, selling our ideas.

> We are about the same size – our income is about $50,000,000 a year.

> We both went international about ten years ago.

> We both derive about half our present billings from outside the U.S.

We are both running out of new countries to enter.

Some of your clients are also clients of ours – like Shell, General Foods, KLM, ICI, American Express.

Of course our two companies are also very different. To name only two differences:

We don't have anything like your up-or-out policy.

You pay your top people more than we do. Only three of our 3500 employees get as much as $100,000 a year.

I can only hope that we have enough in common to give some slight trace of relevance to what I am going to say.

I will begin with an old-fashioned affirmation in the supreme value of *hard work*.

The harder your people work, the happier they will be. I believe in the Scottish proverb: "*Hard work never killed a man.*" Men die of boredom, psychological conflict and disease. They never die of hard work.

I am a stickler for meeting deadlines. I can do almost any job in one weekend. I think everyone can. The trouble is that most chaps are too lazy to burn the midnight oil. They are unwilling to rise to the occasion.

On the other hand, I believe in lots of vacations. When one of my partners gets abrasive, it is usually because he has worked too long without a vacation. I also believe that the partners in a service business should be given sabbaticals to recharge their batteries.

Besides, sabbaticals are fun. Are you guys having any fun? Somebody said to me the other day, "I have never seen a management consultant laugh." Jerome Bruner, the Harvard psychologist, says that he has never visited a lab that was worth a damn where the people weren't having a lot of fun. The physicists at Niels Bohr's lab in Denmark, where they first split the atom, were always playing practical jokes on each other.

... When people aren't having any fun, they seldom produce good work. Kill grimness with laughter. Encourage exuberance. Get rid of sad dogs who spread gloom.

* * * * *

In our kind of business it is awfully difficult to evaluate people in terms of their *performance*. What criteria can we use? "Systematic employee performance ratings?" The evaluations are inevitably subjective. So how can we decide what to pay our senior people?

I am beginning to think that we should follow the example of Winthrop, Stimson, Putnam & Roberts, the law firm. They pay all their partners the *same*, and they have been doing so since the 1880's. They figure that the young partners need as much money as the old ones, and probably more. By paying all the partners the same, they remove the major cause of that sibling rivalry which causes such hellish politics in a service business; they also eliminate the impossible chore of evaluating performance at the partner level.

* * * * *

When a service business grows big, it becomes increasingly difficult to sustain high professional standards. You have to operate systems of quality control. The poor taskmasters have to scrutinize the reports before they go to clients, and most of the time they have to criticize them as superficial, or badly written, or just plain stupid.

This is hell for all concerned, including the taskmaster. He becomes a common scold, an obstructionist to be circumvented – by hook or by crook. The people whose work he excoriates may lose their self-confidence, or sulk, or walk out. It is an odious duty, but is part of "the will to manage."

When a client hires Ogilvy & Mather – or McKinsey – he expects the best. If you don't make sure that he gets it, you shortchange him – and he won't come back for more.

A few years ago I had to draft a report for the British Export Marketing Advisory Committee. I rather fancy myself as a report-writer, and I have exorbitant standards when it comes to criticizing other people's drafts. But this time I got my comeuppance, because one member of our Committee had far higher standards than I had. My God, he gave me a bad time, challenging every bloody paragraph. Guess who. Marvin Bower, that's who.

From a talk to American Express executives, February 1981:

How do you know when you are getting old? It began to dawn on me when the United States elected President Kennedy; he was six years younger than me. Two years ago the Cardinals elected a Pope who is nine years younger than me. Now I am old enough to be your Chairman's father – easily.

When you ask a man of my age to talk, you can be sure of two things. First, that he will talk about the *past*. Second, that he will talk with avuncular candor.

In 1959 John D. Rockefeller III asked me to sell the concept of Lincoln Center to the inhabitants of New York. I had a team of volunteers to help me. The best of those volunteers was a girl called Jean Selden.

Two years later Jean married Howard Clark – and suggested that he might want to hire Ogilvy & Mather. I have spent the subsequent eighteen years trying to justify Jean's advocacy.

The man who was then President of our agency thought I was nuts to take your account. He said it was too small – about a million bucks, which had to cover Cheques, Cards and Travel. He told me, "Jesus Christ could perform a miracle by feeding the multitude with three loaves and two small fishes, but you ain't Jesus Christ."

So I waited for our President to go on vacation, and then signed up …

* * * * *

If I were Chairman of American Express, or head of one of your Divisions, I would keep asking myself eight questions:

(1) Do I encourage my people to bombard me with new ideas? Is the atmosphere around here *creative* and *innovative*, or *dull* and *bureaucratic*? Walter Wriston recently said, "There's no reason you can't have an *innovative* bureaucracy if you put out the word that fame and fortune come from rocking the boat."

　　Creativity and innovation function best in an atmosphere of fun and foment. Creativity hardly functions at all in an atmosphere of politics and fear.

(2) I would ask myself, "Are we operating as a team, as a band of brothers? Or are we competing with each other like silly babies?"

(3) Are we freewheeling entrepreneurs, ready to take risks in new ventures? Or are we too frightened of making mistakes? When the toy-buyer at Sears made a mistake which cost his company 10 million bucks, I asked the head of Sears, "Are you going to fire him?" "Hell no," he replied, "I fire people who *don't* make mistakes."

(4) Are we devoting too much time and money to salvaging our flops, our dry holes – and not enough to exploiting our breakthroughs?

(5) Are we leaders or followers? Do our

TRIUMPHANT GRAPE NUTS

On one of his visits to Chicago, unexpected circumstances caused David to be invited to three dinners in a week at the home of one of his longtime partners.

During the second dinner he carried on at such length about Post Grape Nuts being the ideal main course – "nourishing, easy to digest, doesn't leave you feeling stuffed" – that his hostess felt obliged to put a heaping bowl of this nouvelle cuisine at his place when he showed up a third evening. He ate it with gusto and, back in France, sent her this postcard:

Dearest Marikay,

Never before in all my longish life has anyone else ever invited me to dinner three times in one week. Each dinner was better than the last, culminating in your triumphant Grape Nuts. Thank you, my dear ... Love to you both from your grateful friend,

David

competitors imitate us, or do we imitate them? You may remember Kipling's long poem about Sir Anthony Gloster, the old shipping tycoon. On his deathbed, he is telling his son about his competitors:

"They copied all they could follow,
But they couldn't copy my mind.
And I left 'em sweating and stealing,
A year and a half behind."

(6) Are we trying hard enough to *create new products*? How does our Research & Development compare with Merck, who invested $227 million in R&D last year? That's about eight percent of their sales. IBM invests one billion dollars a year in R&D. In some companies it is easier to get a *hundred* million for an acquisition than *one* million for a new product.

(7) How do we stand with our customers – present and prospective? As long as we are rated tops by the consumers of our products, our position in the marketplace is unassailable ...

(8) What are the Japanese up to? If they can outperform us in electronics and steel and even automobiles, don't be surprised if one day they become a major threat to *your* business. The Japanese have four advantages over us in the West:

A. They take more interest in their employees. They have a saying, "Man, not the bottom line, is the measure of all things." It seems to work.

B. They don't have so many lawyers – *one* lawyer for every 10,000 people in Japan compared with *twenty* lawyers for every 10,000 people in the U.S. (No offense meant, you twenty-one lawyers here tonight.)

C. They don't put their wise men out

to pasture at the age of sixty-five. (This particularly appeals to me.)

D. They aren't so obsessed with short-term profit. Short-term profits? What's so great about short-term profits? I'll tell you. They impress the jackasses on Wall Street. Ten years ago they valued your shares at $40. Today you are making *five times* as much profit, and they value your shares at $43. Can't you find a way to emancipate your company from the stock market? *There's* a challenge!

• • •

From a speech to the 50th Anniversary Luncheon of the Advertising Research Foundation, in New York, March 18, 1986:

SOUND AN ALARM!

... I started my career with George Gallup at Princeton. Gallup contributed more to advertising research than all the rest of us put together. I miss him dreadfully.

When I started Ogilvy & Mather, I wore two hats. On Thursdays and Fridays I was the Research Director. On Mondays, Tuesdays and Wednesdays I was the Creative Director. I was an hermaphrodite. Jekyll and Hyde. The age-old conflict between the Creative function and the Research function was fought out in my throbbing head.

As far as I know, I am the only creative genius who started his career in research. And now, in old age, I have returned to research, my first love. Alex Biel and I have started a Research and Development center within The Ogilvy Group. We are doing basic research, aided and abetted by some universities.

I have always looked at the creative function through the eyes of a researcher – which does not endear me to my fellow copywriters and art directors. And I look at research through the eyes of a copywriter.

Researchers bug me. They use such awful words – like ATTITUDINAL, PARADIGMS, DEMASSIFICATION, RECONCEPTUALIZE, symbiotic linkage and so on. Pretentious bullshit.

They are so infernally *slow*, and their reports are so long. They are masters of NOT INVENTED HERE. One researcher's methodology is another researcher's poison.

Creative types also bug me. They are terrified of research – terrified that it will reveal that their genius is not infallible. They shut their eyes to the body of knowledge that we researchers have built up over the years ...

As a copywriter, what I want from the researchers is to be told what kind of advertising *will make the cash register ring*. A creative person who knows nothing about plus and minus factors, and refuses to learn, may sometimes *luck* into a successful campaign. A blind pig may sometimes find truffles, but it helps to know that they grow under oak trees.

The advertising community is swimming in research

nowadays. It is pouring out of universities, research outfits and advertising agencies. The trouble is that so little of it percolates down to the people on the firing line, like copywriters and art directors. It might be a good idea to declare a five-year moratorium on new research projects while we analyze the huge volume of discoveries that is gathering dust on the shelves.

Advertising is going through a bad period. Commercial clutter is worse than ever. The cost of media is ballooning. The cost of commercial production is scandalous. The problem of client conflicts is driving agencies round the bend. Worst of all, the trend to cut advertising budgets in favor of below-the-line deals is out of control.

The theme of this conclave is the Next 25 Years. I wonder how much advertising there will be 25 years from now? Do you realize what is going on? Manufacturers of package goods are now spending twice as much on below-the-line deals as on advertising. To put it another way, they are spending twice as much on price-cutting as on building brands. Promotion allowances to retailers are now running at $18 billion a year. They have doubled in the last six years.

Manufacturers are buying volume by price discounting, instead of earning it the old-fashioned way – using advertising to build strong brand franchises. As my partner Graham Phillips says, they are *training* consumers to buy on price instead of brand.

Any damn fool can put on a deal, but it takes genius, faith and perseverance to create a brand. The financial rewards do not always come in next quarter's earnings per share, but come they do. When Philip Morris bought General Foods for five billion dollars they were buying *brands*.

There used to be a prosperous brand of coffee called Chase & Sanborn. Then they started dealing. They became *addicted* to price-offs. Where is Chase & Sanborn today? In the cemetery. Dead as a doornail.

I have a habit of prophecy. Listen to three paragraphs from a speech I made to the 4As in 1955 – thirty-one years ago:*

> The manufacturers who dedicate their advertising to building the most favorable image, the most sharply defined *personality* for their brand, are the ones who will get the largest share of market at the highest profit.

> The time has come to *sound an alarm*, to warn our clients what is going to happen to their brands if they spend so much on deals that there is no money left for advertising to build their brand.

> Deals don't build the kind of indestructible image which is the only thing that can make your brand part of the fabric of American life.

I had a client called Bev Murphy. Bev invented Nielsen's technique for measuring consumer purchases, and went on to be President of Campbell Soup Company. I once heard him say:

Editor's Note: Another excerpt from this 1955 speech appears on pages 86–88.

"Promotions cannot produce more than a temporary kink in the sales curve."

Andrew Ehrenberg of the London Business School has one of the best brains in marketing today. Dr. Ehrenberg says:

"A cut-price offer can induce people to try a brand, but they return to their habitual brands as if nothing had happened."

Why are so many brand managers addicted to price-cutting deals? Because the men who employ them are more interested in next quarter's earnings than in building their brands. Why are they so obsessed with next quarter's earnings? Because they are more concerned with their stock options than the future of their company.

Deals are a drug. Ask a drug-addicted brand manager what happens to his share of market after the delirium of the deal subsides. He will change the subject. Try asking him if the deal increased the profit. Again he will change the subject ...

Marketers who have inherited brands built by their predecessors are dealing them to oblivion. Sooner or later they discover that they cannot deal brands which nobody has heard of. May the Lord have mercy on them.

Brands are the seed corn they have inherited. They are eating their seed corn.

These rascals who sell *their* product by cutting the price, expect me to sell *my* product at a cut price. Clients who haggle over agency compensation are looking through the wrong end of the telescope. Instead of trying to shave a few measly dollars off the agencies' 15 percent, they should concentrate on getting more sales results from the 85 percent they invest in time and space. That is where the leverage is. No manufacturer ever got rich by underpaying his agency. Pay peanuts and you get monkeys.

Sound an alarm! Advertising, not deals, builds brands.

Outside his study at Touffou – conducting his worldwide orchestra.

"Principles of Management" and *"Corporate Culture"*

Principles of Management

From a paper written in 1968 as a guide for Ogilvy & Mather managers worldwide:

I have been managing Ogilvy & Mather for twenty years. I have learned from my own mistakes, from the counsel of my partners, from the literature, from George Gallup, Raymond Rubicam and Marvin Bower.

Now I want to share with you what I know about managing Ogilvy & Mather.

I have no desire to impose my personal style on the rest of you. Nor do I seek to freeze the style of Ogilvy & Mather after I retire. I hope that future generations will improve upon the Principles I enunciate in this paper.

• • •

Ogilvy & Mather is not a mere holding company for a group of independent agencies in different countries. It is one agency indivisible.

Our clients must see no basic differences of style between any of our offices. Ogilvy & Mather must never become a company of incompetent amateurs in one country, superb professionals in a second, waffling bumblers in a third.

In this paper, I will set down the principles of management which, in my judgment, are most likely to make our company prosper.

If you endorse these principles, promulgate them, apply them, add to them and revise them during the years to come, our offices will be inspired by *unanimity of purpose*. This will give Ogilvy & Mather a competitive edge over international agencies which lack such unanimity.

Ogilvy & Mather is dedicated to *seven* purposes:

1. To serve our clients more effectively than any other agency.

2. To earn an increased profit every year.

3. To maintain high ethical standards.

4. To run the agency with a sense of competitive urgency.

5. To keep our services up-to-date.

6. To make Ogilvy & Mather the most exciting agency to work in.

7. To earn the respect of the community.

PROFITS

Ogilvy & Mather is in business to earn a profit through superior service to clients.

The Board of Directors agrees on the profit objectives of each office. The governing consideration is the forward thrust of the entire agency.

Profit is not always synonymous with billing. We pursue profit – not billing. The chief opportunities for increasing our profit lie in:

1. Increasing income from present clients.

2. Getting new clients.

3. Separating passengers without delay.

4. Discontinuing boondoggles and obsolete services:

   To keep your ship moving through the water at maximum efficiency, you have to keep scraping the barnacles off its bottom. It is rare for a department head to recommend the abolition of a job, or even the elimination of a man; the pressure from below is always for *adding*. If the initiative for barnacle-scraping does not come from Management, barnacles will never be scraped.

5. Avoiding duplication of function – two men doing a job which one can do.

6. Increasing productivity.

7. Reducing wheel-spinning in the creative area.

8. Putting idle capital to work.

MORALE

Advertising agencies are fertile ground for office politics. You should work hard to minimize them, because they take up energy which can better be devoted to our clients; some agencies have been *destroyed* by internal politics. Here are some ways to minimize them:

1. Always be fair and honest in your own dealings; unfairness and dishonesty at the top can demoralize an agency.

2. Never hire relatives or friends.

3. Sack incurable politicians.

4. Crusade against paper warfare. Encourage your people to air their disagreements *face-to-face*.

5. Discourage secrecy.

6. Discourage poaching.

7. Compose sibling rivalries.

I want all our people to believe that they are working in the best agency in the world. A sense of pride works wonders.

The best way to "install a generator" in a man is to give him the greatest possible responsibility. Treat your subordinates as grown-ups – and they will grow up. Help them when they are in difficulty. Be affectionate and human, not cold and impersonal.

It is vitally important to encourage free communication *upward*. Encourage your people to be candid with you. Ask their advice – and listen to it.

THE FUTURE

At a question-and-answer session after a recent talk, David was asked to comment, from the vantage point of his decades in the business, on the future of advertising.

"I have a diminishing interest in the future," he replied.

Senior men and women have no monopoly on great ideas. Nor do Creative people. Some of the best ideas come from account executives, researchers and others. Encourage this; you need all the ideas you can get.

Encourage innovation. Change is our lifeblood, stagnation our death knell.

Do not summon people to your office – it frightens them. Instead, go to see them in *their* offices. This makes you visible throughout the agency. An office head who never wanders about the agency becomes a hermit, out of touch with the staff.

The physical appearance of our offices is important, because it says so much about Ogilvy & Mather. If they are decorated in bad taste, we are yahoos. If they look old-fashioned, we are fuddy-duddies. If they are too pretentious, we are stuffed shirts. If they are untidy, we are inefficient.

Our offices must look efficient, contemporary, cheerful and functional.

I believe in the Scottish proverb: *Hard work never killed a man*. Men die of boredom, psychological conflict and disease. They do not die of hard work. The harder your people work, the happier and healthier they will be.

Try to make working at Ogilvy & Mather *fun*. When people aren't having any fun, they seldom produce good advertising. Kill grimness with laughter. Maintain an atmosphere of informality. Encourage exuberance. Get rid of sad dogs who spread gloom.

But good morale also requires our top people to be eternally vigilant as to the discipline in their offices. The staff must be made to arrive on time. Telephones must be answered promptly and politely. Filing must be kept up-to-date. Due dates must be kept.

Security must be policed. Indiscretion in elevators and restaurants, premature use of typesetters and Photostat houses, premature display of new campaigns on bulletin boards and indiscreet gossip can do serious damage to our clients and even lose accounts.

It is also the duty of our top people to sustain unremitting pressure on the *professional standards* of their staffs. They must not tolerate sloppy plans or mediocre creative work. In our competitive business, it is suicide to settle for second-rate performance.

Training should not be confined to trainees. It should be a continuous process, and should include the entire professional staff at the agency. The more our people learn, the more useful they can be to our clients.

RESPECT

One of the most priceless assets Ogilvy & Mather can have is the *respect of our clients and of the whole business community*.

This comes from the following:

1. Our offices must always be headed by the kind of people who command respect. Not phonies, zeros or bastards.

2. Always be honest in your dealings with clients. Tell them what you would do if you were in their shoes.

3. If we do a good job for our clients, that will become known. We will smell of success, and that will bring us respect.

4. If we treat our employees well, they will speak well of Ogilvy & Mather to their friends. Assuming that each employee has 100 friends, 250,000 people now have friends who work for Ogilvy & Mather. Among them are present and prospective clients.

5. In meeting with clients, do not assume the posture of servants. They need you as much as you need them.

6. While you are responsible to your clients for sales results, you are also responsible to consumers for the kind of advertising you bring into their homes. Your aim should be to create advertising that is in good taste. I abhor advertising that is blatant, dull, or dishonest. Agencies which transgress this principle are not widely respected.

7.   We must pull our weight as good citizens.

HIRING

The paramount problem you face is this: advertising is one of the most difficult functions in industry, and too few brilliant people want careers in advertising.

The challenge is to recruit people who are able enough to do the difficult work our clients require from us.

1.   Make a conscious effort to avoid recruiting dull, pedestrian hacks.

2.   Create an atmosphere of ferment, innovation and freedom. This will attract brilliant recruits.

If you ever find a man who is better than you are – hire him. If necessary, pay him more than you pay yourself.

In recruitment and promotion we are fanatical in our hatred for all forms of prejudice. We have no prejudice for or against Roman Catholics, Protestants, Negroes, Aristocracy, Jews, Agnostics or foreigners.

PARTNERSHIP

Each Ogilvy & Mather office is a partnership of individual practitioners. Our growth depends on our ability to develop a large cadre of able partners.

Each of our offices has a *managing* partner. The

total responsibility for the office rests on his shoulders. However, if he is wise, he will treat his lieutenants as equals.

If he treats them as subordinates, they will be less effective in their jobs; they will come to resent their subordination – and leave. Only second-raters accept permanent subordination.

For this reason our Top Management in each country should function like a round table, presided over by a managing partner who is big enough to be effective in the role of *primus inter pares*, without having to rely on the overt discipline of a military hierarchy – with its demeaning pecking order.

This egalitarian structure encourages independence, responsibility and loyalty. It reduces the agency's dependence on ONE MAN, who is often fallible, sometimes absent and always mortal. It ensures continuity of style from generation to generation.

No office in the Ogilvy & Mather group has a monopoly on brains. The more we bring the resources of our offices to bear on each other's problems, the better. This requires close liaison at many levels; it also requires that each of our agencies conquer their chauvinism.

If we help each other, the sum of our individual parts will give us a competitive advantage over international agencies which allow iron curtains to separate their offices from each other.

It is as difficult to sustain happy partnerships as to sustain happy marriages. The challenge can be met if those concerned practice these restraints:

1. Have clear-cut divisions of responsibility.

2. Don't poach on the other fellow's preserves.

3. Live and let live; nobody is perfect.

4. "Why beholdest thou the mote that is in thy brother's eye, but considerest not the beam that is in thine own eye?"

ISLANDS OF LEADERSHIP

It is impossible for our office heads to carry the whole load of *leadership* single-handed. Their partners and department heads must be islands of leadership – inspiring, explaining, disciplining and counseling.

It is not enough for people at this level to concern themselves only with their professional function; they must also be leaders.

In selecting heads of service departments, it is not always wise to select those whose professional qualifications are the best; outstanding professionals do not always turn out to be good *leaders*. It is often better to give management jobs on the basis of *leadership* ability, leaving the professionals to practice their profession.

This is particularly true in the creative area. Some of the best copywriters and art directors make poor Creative Directors. If you give them recognition in terms of salary and glory, you can persuade them to let others pass them on the administrative ladder, while they continue to create the campaigns on which the whole agency depends.

136

COMERS

The management of manpower resources is one of the most important duties of our office heads. It is particularly important for them to spot people of unusual promise early in their careers, and to move them up the ladder as fast as they can handle increased responsibility.

There are five characteristics which suggest to me that a person has the potential for rapid promotion:

1. *He is ambitious.*

2. *He works harder than his peers – and enjoys it.*

3. *He has a brilliant brain – inventive and unorthodox.*

4. *He has an engaging personality.*

5. *He demonstrates respect for the creative function.*

If you fail to recognize, promote and reward young people of exceptional promise, they will leave you; the loss of an exceptional man can be as damaging as the loss of an account.

CREATIVE PEOPLE

I think that the creative function is the most important of all. The heads of our offices should not relegate their key creative people to positions below the salt. They should pay them, house them and respect them as indispensable Stars.

MANAGEMENT SUPERVISORS

I respect the value of Management Supervisors. At their best, they keep the agency out of turbulence; keep service costs under control; emancipate the office heads from perpetual fire-fighting; and stimulate our service departments to do good work for clients, thus winning new business of the most profitable kind.

Our Management Supervisors are equivalent to the partners in great law firms. They must be stable, courageous, persuasive, professional and imaginative. They must work in fruitful partnership with our creative people – neither bullying them nor knuckling under to them.

Above all, they must have the thrust of independent entrepreneurs. This is not a job for lazy, frightened mediocrities; nor is it a job for superficial "contact" men.

Intellectual snobbery towards clients is common – and dangerous. When a Management Supervisor comes to regard his client as a boob, he should be transferred to another account. While our clients may not always be good judges of advertising, their jobs are broader than ours; they have to encompass areas about which we are ignorant – research and development, production, logistics, sales management, labor relations, etc.

TREASURERS

I respect the importance of our Treasurers. They must carry the guns to make their voices heard in our management councils. They must be tough and unafraid. They must be privy to all our secrets – and they must be discreet.

RESEARCHERS

No agency has greater respect for the importance of the research function – particularly in the creative area. The most valuable quality in a Research Director is his scientific integrity. A dishonest Research Director can do appalling damage to any agency.

It is also important that a Research Director be able to work sympathetically with our creative people.

And he should be able to use research *fast* and *cheaply*.

NEW BUSINESS

The most difficult decisions which confront our managements are decisions as to which accounts to take and which to reject. The primary considerations should be:

1. Does anyone in Top Management really *want* the account? We should never take an account unless at least one key man can approach it with enthusiasm.

2. Can good advertising sell the product? It does not pay to take on terminal cases.

3. Would it be a *happy marriage*? Unhappy marriages do not fructify – and do not last.

139

4. Will the account contribute significantly to our profits? Has it significant *potential for growth*?

5. If we take this account will it risk losing us another account – anywhere?

6. Will the account involve heavy risks? An account that bills more than 30 percent of the total billing in an office places the whole office at risk, and this is irresponsible. (In the early days of a new office, it makes sense to accept this risk.)

Try to avoid new business contests when the prospective client is going to publish the names of the contenders. Only one agency can win; the others will be publicly branded as failures. We like to succeed in public, to fail in private.

The best way to get new accounts is to create for our *present* clients the kind of advertising that will attract *prospective* clients.

We do not have New Business departments in our offices. No first-class man will take the job; no second-class man can do it effectively.

The prime responsibility for new business must lie with heads of offices. They should not allow Management Supervisors to spend too much time in this area; their prime responsibility must always be to our present clients.

* * * * *

POLITICAL ACCOUNTS

We do not handle political party accounts. Our reasons are:

1. They preempt too much of the time of our top men, thereby causing trouble with our permanent clients.

2. When an agency espouses one party, it is unfair to those of our people who are rooting for the other party.

3. By identifying the agency with one party, we would incur the enmity of important people in the other party; we cannot afford this.

However, good citizenship requires us to encourage our people to participate in political life – *in their private capacity*.

In the same way, we applaud when they make their special skills available to charitable causes.

It is reasonable for our office heads to involve their offices in helping non-political charities which are of special interest to them.

WHEN TO RESIGN AN ACCOUNT

If you resign accounts every time you feel like doing so, you will empty your portfolio every year. However, there are two circumstances in which resignation is the wisest choice:

1. When the agency would be more profitable without the account; this is uncommon.

2. When the client bullies the agency to such an extent that the morale of your staff is seriously impaired and starts hurting their performance on other accounts.

REMUNERATION BY FEE

In all countries where it is legal, we offer clients a choice of fee or commission. Fees offer five advantages over commissions:

1. The agency can be more objective in its recommendations; or so many clients believe.

2. The agency has adequate incentive to provide non-commissionable services if needed.

3. The agency's income is stabilized. Unforeseen cuts in advertising expenditure do not result in red figures or temporary personnel layoffs.

4. The fee enables the agency to make a fair profit on services rendered. The advertiser, in turn, pays for what he gets – no more, no less.

5. Every fee account pays its own way. Unprofitable accounts do not ride on the coattails of profitable accounts.

Then there is the commission system, and some clients prefer it.

Both systems will continue for years to come. We should be open-minded about our use of them.

Corporate Culture

A dinner address to the Directors of The Ogilvy Group, and to the heads of a number of The Group's agencies, in London at Fishmongers Hall, June 1985:

Three years ago Terrence Deal and Allen Kennedy wrote a book about corporate culture. They said:

"The people who built the companies for which America is famous, all worked obsessively *to create strong cultures within their organizations.*

"Companies that have cultivated their individual identities by shaping values, making heroes, spelling out rites and rituals, and acknowledging the cultural networking *have an edge.*"

Now the concept of corporate culture has caught on in a big way, not only in the U.S.A., but also in England. In a recent article, Frances Cairncross of *The Economist* wrote, "The common characteristic of success is the deliberate creation of a corporate culture."

I have been wondering if Ogilvy & Mather has a corporate culture. *Apparently we do.*

The head of one of the biggest agencies recently told us, "Yours is the only agency in the world with a real corporate culture."

We seem to have an exceptionally <u>strong</u> culture. Indeed, it may be this, more than anything else, which differentiates us from our competitors.

It occurred to me that it might be a good idea to write it down. I have put it in the form of a letter to Bill Phillips. He has asked me to read it aloud to you. Here goes.

Dear Bill:

You have asked me to describe our corporate culture as I see it.

Corporate culture is a compound of many things – *tradition, mythology, ritual, customs, habits, heroes, peculiarities,* and *values*.

Here is how I see *our* culture.

A NICE PLACE TO WORK

Some of our people spend their entire working lives in our agency. We do our damnedest to make it a *happy* experience. I put this first, believing that superior service to our clients and profits for our stockholders depend on it.

We treat our people like human beings. We help them when they are in trouble – with their jobs, with illness, with alcoholism, and so on.

We help our people make the best of their talents. We invest an awful lot of time and money in training – perhaps more than any of our competitors.

Our system of management is singularly democratic.

RUSSIAN DOLLS
(from an interview)

OGILVY: When you hire people from outside, it's very important how you do it. We had a board meeting some time ago, and every director had at his place one of these Russian dolls.

I said: "That's you. Open it."

So they opened the doll, and inside was a smaller one. And they opened it up and each doll got smaller and smaller. And finally, when they got to the very inside, in the smallest doll they found a tiny piece of paper on which I had written a motto.

When they unfolded it, it said: "If you always hire people who are smaller than you are, we shall become a company of dwarfs. If, on the other hand, you always hire people who are bigger than you are, we shall become a company of giants."

We don't like hierarchical bureaucracy or rigid pecking orders.

We abhor ruthlessness.

We give our executives an extraordinary degree of freedom and independence.

We like people with *gentle manners*. Our New York office goes so far as to give an annual award for "professionalism combined with *civility*." The Jules Fine Award, named after the first winner.

We like people who are *honest*. Honest in argument, honest with clients, honest with suppliers, honest with the company – and above all, honest with consumers.

We admire people who work hard, who are objective and thorough.

We do *not* admire superficial people.

We despise office politicians, toadies, bullies and pompous asses.

We discourage paper warfare. The way up the ladder is open to everybody. We are free from prejudice of any kind – religious prejudice, racial prejudice or sexual prejudice.

We detest nepotism and every other form of favouritism.

In promoting people to top jobs, we are influenced as much by their *character* as anything else.

Like all companies with a strong culture, we have our *heroes* – the Old Guard who have woven our culture. By no means have all of them been members of top management. They include people like Borgie, our immortal Danish typographer. Shelby Page, who was our Treasurer and Chief Iconoclast in New York for 34 years. Arthur Wilson, the roving English art director who is the funniest man in our history. Paul Biklen, who has shepherded thousands of us through training programs. And Joel Raphaelson, editor of *Viewpoint*, veteran copywriter, lanternist, and ghost-writer extraordinary.

ATTITUDE TOWARDS CLIENTS

The recommendations we make to clients are the recommendations we would make if we owned their companies, without regard to our own short-term interest. This earns their *respect*, which is the greatest asset an agency can have.

What most clients want from agencies is *superior*

A MATTER OF UNIMPORTANCE

One Vice President, ambitious to become a Senior Vice President, had a meeting with David on a number of matters. He brought along a typed agenda. The last item was *Senior Vice Presidency*.

With a couple of points still to go, something urgent came up and brought the meeting to an abrupt end. The Vice President left, forgetting his agenda, which David found later and returned to him with a handwritten note:

"I believe we covered all the important items."

---

creative work. We put the creative function at the top of our priorities.

The line between *pride in our work* and *neurotic obstinacy* is a narrow one. We do not grudge clients the right to decide what advertising to run. It is their money.

Many of our clients employ us in several countries. It is important for them to know that they can expect the same standards of behavior in all our offices. That is one reason why we want our culture to be more or less the same everywhere.

We try to sell our clients' products without offending the mores of the countries where we do business. And without cheating the consumer.

We attach important to *discretion*. Clients don't appreciate agencies which leak their secrets. Nor do they like it when an agency takes credit for *their* success. To get between a client and the footlights is bad manners.

We take new business very seriously, and have a passion for winning. But we play fair vis-à-vis our competitors.

PECULIARITIES

Our far-flung enterprise is held together by a network of personal friendships. We all belong to the same club.

We like reports and correspondence to be well written, easy to read – and *short*.

We are revolted by pseudo-academic jargon, like attitudinal, paradigms, demassification, reconceptualise, suboptimal, symbiotic linkage, splinterisation, dimensionalisation.

Some of us write books.

We use the word *partner* in referring to each other. This says a mouthful.

We take our Christmas get-togethers seriously. On these elaborate occasions we take our entire staff into our confidence – and give them a rollicking good time.

When we opened the New York office in 1948, I had it painted battleship grey. The result was depressing, so I changed to white walls and red carpets. Most of our offices are still white and red.

EX CATHEDRA

Through maddening repetition, some of my *obiter dicta* have been woven into our culture. Here are ten of them:

1. "Ogilvy & Mather – one agency indivisible."

2. "We sell – or else."

3. "You cannot *bore* people into buying your product; you can only *interest* them in buying it."

4. "Raise your sights! Blaze new trails" "Compete with the immortals!!!"

5. "I prefer the discipline of knowledge to the anarchy of ignorance. We pursue

knowledge the way a pig pursues truffles."

6. "We hire gentlemen with brains."

7. "The consumer is not a moron. She is your wife. Don't insult her intelligence."

8. "Unless your campaign contains a Big Idea, it will pass like a ship in the night."

9. "Only First Class business, and that in a First Class way."

10. "Never run an advertisement you would not want your own family to see."

AS OTHERS SEE US

This letter describes our culture as I see it. How do outsiders see it? A recent survey among advertisers and other agencies revealed that our New York office is seen as "sophisticated, imaginative, disciplined, objective and exciting." This describes exactly the culture I have devoted 36 years to cultivating.

The head of another agency recently told us, "You are not only the leaders of our industry, you are gentlemen, you are teachers and you make us proud to be in the advertising business."

David

In Houston in 1980.

"Leadership: The Forgotten Factor in Management"

Leadership

The Charles Coolidge Parlin Memorial Lecture,

Philadelphia, May 10, 1972:

Charles Coolidge Parlin was the father of market research, but only five of the thirty-two men who have received the Parlin Award have been *researchers*. I am proud to be one of them.

I started my career in this country with George Gallup at Princeton, and I owe him more than I owe any other man.

Nowadays I earn my living in the advertising business. However, I am not going to talk about advertising this evening. To tell you the truth, I have nothing to say on the subject that I have not said elsewhere – and it seems to me that the least a recipient of the Parlin Award can do is to say something which he hasn't said before.

After advertising, the subject which interests me most nowadays is *leadership*. I have discovered that when Ogilvy & Mather appoints good leaders to manage our offices, everything blossoms. When we appoint a poor leader, everything withers.

For the last 24 years, I have had unique opportunities

for observing the men who manage great corporations. Most of them are fine *problem-solvers* and *decision-makers*, but relatively few of them seem to be outstanding *leaders*. Some of them, far from inspiring their lieutenants, display a genius for castrating them.

ELECTRIFYING

It has been my observation that great leadership can have an electrifying effect on the performance of any corporation. Perhaps the best leader I have encountered in corporate life was General Wood of Sears, Roebuck.

In my own trade, the best leaders I have observed have been Raymond Rubicam, Leo Burnett and Bill Bernbach.

I have had the good fortune to work for three superb leaders – Monsieur Pitard, my old boss in the kitchens of the Majestic Hotel in Paris; George Gallup; and Sir William Stephenson of British Intelligence.

There has been a huge amount of social science research into leadership. Twelve years ago, a summary of the literature cited 111 references.

It is the consensus among the social scientists that success in leadership depends on the circumstances. For example, a man who has been an outstanding leader in an industrial company is sometimes a flop when he goes to Washington as Secretary of Commerce.

The kind of leadership which works well in a young struggling company seldom works well in a large, mature company.

ACADEMIC ACHIEVEMENT NOT ESSENTIAL

There appears to be no correlation between industrial leadership and high academic achievement. I was relieved to learn this, because I have no college degree, still less an MBA. It appears that the motivation which makes a man a good student is not the kind of motivation which makes a man a good leader.

There is a tendency for corporations to reject executives who do not fit their conventions. How many corporations today would promote an unorthodox maverick like Charlie Kettering of General Motors? I suggest that corporations should try to tolerate and encourage their mavericks. The best leaders are apt to be found among those executives who have a strong component of unorthodoxy in their characters. Instead of resisting innovation, they symbolize it – and companies seldom grow without innovation.

Great leaders almost seem to exude *self-confidence*.

They are never petty. They are *big* men. They are never buck passers.

They are resilient, they pick themselves up after defeat – in the way that Howard Clark picked himself up after the salad oil swindle in his company. Under his indomitable leadership, the price of American Express shares has increased fourteen fold since that swindle.

GUTS

Great industrial leaders are always fanatically committed to their jobs. They are not lazy, or amateurs.

POLICY GAP

It used to be the policy of the agency, when employees married each other, that one of them had to leave. (In those days it wasn't against the law.) A month or so before the wedding of one such couple, David explained to them why this was a good policy, in their own interest as well as the company's.

Warming to the subject, he reminisced about two other employees who, years before, had shared living quarters out of wedlock while both continued to work at the agency. He hadn't much cared for that, from a business point of view. *"But you see,"* he said, *"I couldn't do anything about it because we don't have any agency policy against living in sin."*

They do not suffer from the crippling need to be universally loved; they have the guts to make unpopular decisions – including the guts to fire non-performers.

Gladstone once said that a great Prime Minister must be a good butcher. The only President in recent years who has had the guts to fire people was Harry Truman. He was a great leader within his Cabinet.

I saw my old boss in the kitchens of the Hotel Majestic fire one of his chefs because the poor devil could not get his brioches to rise straight. I was shocked by this ruthlessness, but it made all the other chefs feel that they were working in the best kitchen in the world. Their morale would have done credit to the U.S. Marine Corps.

I have observed that some men are good at leading

the multitude – whether it be the labor force in their company, or the voting population in their country. They are inspiring demagogues, and that can be valuable. But these same men are often miserable leaders of their cabinet or their inside group of executives.

Good leaders are *decisive*. They grasp nettles.

DRINK

Some of them are very odd characters indeed. Lloyd George was sexually chaotic. General Grant, who won the Civil War, drank like a fish. On November 26, 1863, the New York Herald quoted Lincoln as saying:

> *"I wish some of you would tell me the brand of whiskey that Grant drinks. I would like to send a barrel of it to my other generals."*

Winston Churchill drank as much as Grant. He was capricious and petulant. He was grossly inconsiderate to his staff. He was a colossal egotist. Yet his chief of staff wrote of him:

> *"I shall always look back on the years I worked with him as some of the most difficult and trying ones in my life. For all that I thank God that I was given the opportunity of working alongside such a man, and of having my eyes opened to the fact that occasionally such supermen exist on this earth."*

I do not believe that *fear* is a component in a good leadership. It has been my observation that executives do their best work, and certainly their most creative work, in a happy atmosphere. Ferment and innovation thrive in an atmosphere of *joie de vivre*.

FUN

Jerome Bruner, the Harvard psychologist, says that there has never been a great scientific laboratory where the people weren't having *fun*. The physicists who split the atom in Niels Bohr's lab were always playing practical jokes on each other.

I am indebted to my friend and erstwhile competitor Charlie Brower for his amendment to the first verse in the thirteenth chapters of St Paul's first Epistle to the Corinthians, "A man who spendeth his life gathering gold for the United States Treasury and has no fun, is a sounding ass and a tinkling idiot."

The great leaders I have known have been curiously *complicated* men. Howard Johnson, the former President of M.I.T., has described this trait as "a visceral form of spiritual energy which provides the element of *mystery* in leadership."

I have seen this visceral form of spiritual energy, this element of mystery, in Marvin Bower of McKinsey, in Ted Moscoso of Puerto Rico, in the late Henry Alexander of Morgan Guaranty.

AMERICAN LEADERSHIP NOT EXPORTABLE

There are three facets of the leadership phenomenon – the *leader*, the *followers* and the *situation*.

The most effective leader is the one who satisfies the psychological needs of his followers.

For example, it is one thing to be a good leader of Americans, who are raised in a tradition of democracy and have a high need for independence. But the American brand of democratic leadership doesn't work so well in Europe. European executives are more *dependent* than Americans; they have a psychological need for *autocratic* leadership.

That is one reason why it is usually wise for American corporations to appoint natives to lead their foreign subsidiaries – natives are more successful in leading other natives.

In a situation of *crisis*, it is difficult to lead in a democratic way. When pressures are less urgent, it is easier for the leader to involve his subordinates in the decision-making process.

It does a company no good when its leader *never* shares his leadership functions with his lieutenants. The more centers of leadership you find in a company, the stronger it will become.

BEING A GOOD FOLLOWER

There is an art in being a good *follower*. On the night before a major battle, Winston Churchill's ancestor, the first Duke of Marlborough, was reconnoitering the ground. He and his staff were on horseback. Marlborough dropped his glove. Cadogan, his chief of staff, dismounted, picked up the glove and handed it back to Marlborough. The other officers thought this remarkably civil of Cadogan. Later that evening, Marlborough issued his final order: "Cadogan, put a battery of guns where I dropped my glove."

"I have already done so," replied Cadogan.

He had read Marlborough's mind, and anticipated his order. Cadogan was the kind of follower that makes leadership easy. I have known men whom *nobody* could lead.

Leadership is out of fashion nowadays. As William Shirer said the other day, "the mass of people are skeptical of a great man, especially one with a great mind. They would rather vote for someone who is mediocre, like themselves."

YOU CAN LEARN TO LEAD

It isn't always a disaster when a mediocre man is put into a leadership position. The social scientists agree with me that a man can *learn* the art of leadership – if he thinks it important to try, and if he has sufficiently long tenure at the top. I myself am not a good leader, but I'm a little better than I was when I first reached the top in my company.

It is horribly difficult to *predict* whether a man will be a good leader if he is given the chance. The psychologists in OSS came close to making a science of predicting leadership, but very few corporations take enough pains in this areas.

I believe that it is more important for a leader in today's world to be trained in *psychiatry* than in *cybernetics*. The head of a big company recently said to me,

"I am no longer a Chairman. I have had to become a psychiatric nurse." Today's executive is under pressures which were unknown to the last generation.

I heard Dr. William Menninger lecture on this subject. He said:

> *"The boss is inevitably a father figure. To be a good father requires that he be understanding, that he be considerate, and that he be human enough to be affectionate.*

> *"One of the most important jobs in life for all of us is to be a good listener. So much of the art of communication is the ability to listen, which has so much to do with motivating people."*

GHOSTWRITERS

Most of the great leaders I have known had the ability to inspire people with their *speeches*. If you cannot write inspiring speeches yourself, use ghostwriters – but use *good* ones. Roosevelt used Archibald MacLeish, Robert Sherwood and Judge Rosenman. That is why his speeches were more inspiring than those of any of the Presidents we have had since. "The only thing we have to fear is fear itself."

Very few of the business leaders I know are good on their feet – whoever writes their speeches, and however well they are written, the boss delivers them atrociously. This art can be learned, by anyone who takes the trouble to learn it. In these days of electioneering on television, almost all major politicians have the sense to hire experts to teach them the art of delivery.

The man who has said the wisest things about leadership is, in my opinion, Field Marshal Montgomery. He has said:

> *"The leader must have infectious optimism, and the determination to persevere in the face of difficulties. He must also radiate confidence, even when he himself is not too certain of the outcome.*

> *"The final test of a leader is the feeling you have when you leave his presence after a conference. Have you a feeling of uplift and confidence?"*

The Duke of Wellington, who won the battle of Waterloo, used to say that Napoleon's presence on the battlefield was worth 40,000 soldiers.

Ladies and Gentlemen, I ask you to forgive me for this excursion outside my field of competence. Tomorrow morning, I shall return to my job – which is writing advertisements. That is my trade. That is my profession. But unforeseen circumstances have catapulted me into a position where I also have to function as a leader.

Like so many businessmen, I have been promoted above the level of my competence.

In his beloved garden at Touffou.

David Ogilvy at 75
An interview at his home in France

David Ogilvy at 75
An interview at his home in France

David's 75th birthday was June 23, 1986. Two weeks earlier Joel Raphaelson interviewed him at his home in France, for Viewpoint, *the Ogilvy & Mather magazine. Some of the things he said came as a surprise even to long-time associates. Here are excepts from three and a half hours of tapes.*

❧   ❧   ❧

You've spent about half your life so far in advertising. During the first half of your life did you have any notion what the second half would be like?

No. During the first half of my life I expected to go into politics, which meant Parliament in England. Pretty vague ambition, but that's the way I saw my future.

Whenever I was in London I always went to the House of Commons in the evening, sat in the gallery and listened to debates. One day I was in the gallery in the House of Commons in London, I don't know how old I was, say 35, and I was listening to them that night and looking at them. And I suddenly said to myself, I don't want it. I'd lost interest. That's not for me.

Then I started an advertising agency.

Before you started the agency, did you have ambition in the conventional sense of wanting to be rich and famous or powerful in some or other?

I had two ambitions. One was to have a Rolls-Royce and the other was to have a knighthood. And I got the Rolls-Royce but never got the knighthood.

I got over the Rolls-Royce. I've got a Volkswagen now. I came pretty close to the knighthood. I got the CBE, Commander of the British Empire. If I'd got the one above that, these things are stratified, it would have been a K, which would have been a knighthood. I didn't get that.

You've written a lot about various events in your life, but how they came about, that's a little hazy sometimes. For instance, what got you from Oxford to working in a kitchen in Paris?

You see the great failure of my life was Oxford. I was supposed to be a star at Oxford. And instead of that, I was thrown out. I couldn't pass the exams.

Why? Didn't you study?

I don't know why. I'd like to know. I don't know to this day. I'll die not knowing. I think something happened to me. I had a very serious operation, two of them, on my head and maybe that was it. That sounds like an excuse. Anyway, I screwed that up and I got thrown out.

What happened to your head?

I had double mastoids. I had my head swathed in bandages for a year. Anyway that was the big failure of my life. It would be awful for any student. But for a star Oxford student, it was really dreadful.

They thought I was going to be an historian, you know. So I ran away from that sort of cultural background and became a workman, a cook – as far away from that fancy thing as I possibly could.

Did you go to work as a cook in England or did you go straight to France?

I went straight to France and managed to get a job in a kitchen in Paris. It was terribly hard work. I worked six days a week. I worked 63 hours a week, standing up, appalling heat, frightful pressure and paid almost nothing.

One day a man came to Paris who was the sales manager for Aga Cookers, Aga stoves. He was looking for someone to sell Aga stoves to restaurants and hotels in England. He offered me the job.

Why did he look in Paris for someone to sell stoves in England?

He wanted someone who could speak French to the French chefs in London. So I went back and started selling Agas in England.

So you could speak French then?

Kitchen French. I'd talk to chefs in their own language, which is a very peculiar and rather dirty language.

Why do you live in France now?

I was brought up in England. I first started coming to France when I was about 14. I always loved it. I had a wonderful time in France. I thought it was the most interesting country. And then, when I grew up and left the University, I went to live in

Château de Touffou

Paris and became a cook and that was a wonderful experience for me.

And then for years when I lived in New York, I quite often spent my summer vacation in France and went on bicycle tours. I've always loved being in France. I really don't know why, but I always have.

I happen to like a lot of French people. I love the landscape. I'm a gardener and it's a good country for gardening in. I like the small scale of the towns.

But you know, most of the important decisions you make in life, at least that I make, I haven't the faintest idea why I make them. I can produce a lot of rationalizations for some emotional thing very deep in my subconscious. So if you ask me why do I live in France, I suppose the answer is I haven't the faintest idea.

What would you have done different if you could do it all over?

The first thing that comes to mind is that I wouldn't have made so damn many mistakes, and most notably, I would not have sold so many of my Ogilvy & Mather shares.

There was a time when I owned 30 percent of the company. Well, it was the only thing I had in the world, 30 percent of this advertising agency, which wasn't very big in those days.

I was scared. We were being fantastically successful. I kept saying to myself: easy come, easy go. This thing could go up in smoke at any moment. I was frightened and I wanted to get the money out and put it into something safe, like tax exempts.

So whenever I could sell shares, I did. And it had one good aspect to it. It got some shares into the hands of other people.

But you know, every time I sold my shares, the price of the shares went up. I kept on selling them. If I had all the shares I'd originally had, I would be worth an enormous fortune today.

What was your hardest decision?

Well, I suppose about the hardest decisions have been firing people.

Other very important decisions, perhaps the most important decisions, might be called merger decisions. We were frequently asked to merge with other agencies. Always much bigger than we were. It's a polite word, merger. They were really trying to buy us. And I had to decide whether to do it or not.

The first one was Interpublic. Marion Harper tried to acquire us and offered us half-a-million dollars for our agency and I decided not to do it.

When was that?

I think about 1955, somewhere in there. Very early on.

And then J. Walter Thompson tried twice to buy us, to merge with us, and I decided not to do it.

BBDO wanted to merge with us when they were about five times as big as we were. Foote, Cone & Belding tried to get us. Leo Burnett tried to merge with us. Leo's idea was that we would become their New York end.

I refused all of those. Those weren't very easy decisions to make. Sometimes. Awfully flattering, you know, those invitations were.

I guess the real fundamental reason was a rather personal one. I liked Ogilvy & Mather and I didn't want to muddle it up with anybody else. I thought we were a marvelous outfit. I liked the atmosphere. We were doing well. Relatively successful. We did good advertising campaigns. We were very creative.

There was, of course, a measure of egotism in this. I didn't want to have my philosophies diluted by other people's philosophies. (We called it philosophy. Nowadays it's called corporate culture.) I thought we'd got the best damn agency and we'd go a long way and do very well and all have happy lives if we just stayed where we were and not get into bed with a bunch of strangers whose corporate culture, in many cases, was so different from ours.

Leo Burnett – I thought he'd wear me out if we merged. I was always a fairly hard worker, but nothing like Leo. I thought, my God, he'd call me, if we got into bed with him, he'd call me from Chicago at midnight, wake me up, say meet me in Detroit at 8 o'clock tomorrow morning because we're going to solicit the DeSoto or some automobile account. And I'd have to go there as a good partner. I couldn't stand that.

But the fundamental reason was that I liked Ogilvy &
Mather. I thought it was in the process of becoming the best
damn agency in the history of the world. And I didn't want to
muddle it up with any other agency.

Do you care to comment on the megamergers?

I'd like to comment, yes.

I have so often resisted the temptation to megamerge myself.
When other people start doing it, I still am glad I resisted it.

Megamergers are for megalomaniacs. Megalomaniacs make
megamergers. The people who make megamergers are the
people who want to be the head of the biggest goddamn advertising agency. That's their ambition. That's what they want.

These big mergers do nothing for the people in the agency.
It's quite the opposite. They do nothing for their clients. And
it remains to be seen whether they do anything for stockholders. What they do good for is the megalomaniacs who engineer
them. So I'm against that.

How would you describe your role in the company today?

It's kind of hard to define. I am a director of the company. My
advice is asked. And when it's asked, I give it. I sometimes give
advice when it's not asked, which causes a certain amount of
irritation to the people I give it to.

I don't like my present role as much as I liked my active role.
It used to be that when I went to see clients I'd got something
in my hand to show them – an ad or a layout or a storyboard or
research report or something. I was doing business with them
and I was earning my living.

It isn't like that any longer. Now I'm so often taken to see clients like a sort of exhibit at the zoo.

But I'm in this particular position today. There have been some major figures in the history of advertising. Particularly American advertising. People like Albert Lasker and Stanley Resor of Thompson and in a sense Ray Rubicam. I belong to that group and I'm the last of them. It's an endangered species. Resor is gone. Retired and then died. Bernbach is dead. Rubicam is dead. Ben Duffy of BBDO is dead.

They've all gone and I'm the lone survivor and I happen to be thought of as a creative man. I am a sort of symbol of creativity. A lot of the younger creative people don't think so, but the fact is that in the great world at large, I am that.

There's some advantage to the company in having the last surviving symbolic figure around, I think. It helps to differentiate our agency, our company, from other agencies. Bill Phillips, who's the head of our company and a very active head, feels this quite strongly. He thinks I have some value to the company and that he can make good use of me. Which he does and I love being made use of.

Sometimes I disagree with Bill. Occasionally there'll be an issue, sometimes quite an important one, and I disagree with him. I never know whether it's my duty to keep my disagreement to myself or to argue. And in fact, I do argue with him sometimes. And he could say, "Shut up, I'm running this agency now – you're not. You keep quiet and if I want to do it, your duty is to help me and support me."

He doesn't take that position. He does want to know what I really think on these issues. And on those rare occasions – they aren't many, but there have been two or three of them – that I have disagreed with him quite strongly, I've said so and he's never shown the slightest sign of resentment. And I salute him for that and I'm grateful to him for that.

I have one other asset for the company. I have no axe to grind now. Beyond giving advice or a strong opinion on an issue, I've never got a vested interest in the result. It's sometimes quite difficult to find directors who have no vested interest in policy.

If you believe in reincarnation, what will you come back as?

I might come back as one of those turtles in the Galápagos, because they live so long. You know there's a turtle called George in the Galápagos which was alive in the 18th century. It's the last of its species. When it dies, there'll be no more of that kind of turtle. I might come back as a Galápagos turtle.

I don't know. They may lead rather dull lives – long, but they can't be interesting.

I'd like to come back as a concert pianist. That would be fun. I wouldn't mind being Pope either. Nobody would argue with me if I were Pope.

Did you ever think the agency was going to fail?

Yes. Every day for years I thought it was going to fail. I was always scared sick – always a terrible worrywart when I was in my heyday at the agency.

I always thought our clients were going to fire us, and all our best people were going to leave. The tragedy of it. We were doing so well, I should have been bursting with happiness and satisfaction with all that success. In fact I was tortured with anxiety. I remember saying one day: If this is success, God deliver me from failure.

So I was always terrified. And it wasn't till fairly recent years that it dawned on me we were unlikely to go up in smoke. We'd become an institution. We might do better in the future, we might do worse, but we were not going to fail.

So then I relaxed. But by that time it was rather too late for me to get much pleasure out of it.

In the early years, in spite of being terrified, you resigned a lot of accounts. Why? Was there a pattern to the reasons?

There were two main things. In those days I had to deal direct with the clients. We only had one office and about 18 clients and I dealt directly with all of them. Personal dislike made me resign many accounts. I didn't like having to deal with the sonofabitch. Why should I? We pass this way only once.

Then when clients were demoralizing our people. I went to see the head of _____, a man I liked very much. I said I've come to resign your business. He asked why. I said because your Executive Vice President is a shit. And he's behaving very badly. He's treating *your* people atrociously and he's treating *my* people atrociously. Now what he does to your people – that's your business. But I'm not going to allow this man to go on demoralizing the people of Ogilvy & Mather. It's something I won't accept. So goodbye.

And I resigned products that didn't work, like Rolls-Royce. That's why I resigned the Rolls-Royce account. They went through a very bad two-year period. I wrote to them one day and said – I put the heading "Lemons" on my letter (I don't know if I stole that from the Volkswagen advertising) – I said that the last 600 cars you sent to the United States don't work. And I will no longer be a party to recommending that people buy them. I resign.

How did you find out the cars didn't work?

Because I knew all about it. I knew what was going on. Automatic gears had just come in and their automatic gearbox didn't work. So they had to go and buy one from Chrysler which did work.

And then they put in air conditioning for Americans and other people who lived in hot countries. They sent six cars over with air conditioning in them. The manager of the American company went down and got these new air-conditioned Rolls-Royces off the boat.

The first one he drove around Central Park. He didn't go halfway around Central Park before the windows fogged up. He couldn't see out. Things like that happened all the time.

I wrote this dreadful letter resigning. Even then I thought I was dreadful. Now I think it was unpardonably offensive. But you know they didn't take offense at all. The head of Rolls-Royce, who was an engineer, wrote back and said I don't blame you at all. I think you have a point.

For the next few years, whenever they got in a jam they used to come and ask my advice.

Anything you've always wanted that eluded you?

A knighthood. I told you about that. A big family. Ten children.

You've often given advice to young people about values, how to get ahead, and so on. What about older people in advertising, facing retirement?

Retiring can be fatal, whether it's retiring voluntarily or getting sacked. At any age.

If you find yourself being fired or quitting when you're 50ish, it's so often that you've been working in a job that you don't really like and are probably not any good at. If you were any good at it, you wouldn't be let go.

It's tragic to see men and women wasting their lives in work that they hate or do badly. It's never too late to find out that you're doing something you don't like, and are not very good at. Then you've got to take hold of yourself and decide what you would like to be doing most and then do it for the rest of your life.

There's a man called Guy Mountfort, who was for a year or two the Managing Director of what is now our London office. He got to be about 55, 54, and the question was whether he was going to go on. He wanted to go on and I advised him not to go on.

I said to him, you watch the clock in the office. You're waiting for 5 o'clock when you can go home and do what you really love, which is being an ornithologist. We ad men are a dime a dozen. You ornithologists are rare birds. Go and do it and be happy. And he did it. He retired.

He's done marvelous work. He was one of the founders of the World Wildlife Fund. He got me into it. He's almost single-handedly saved the tiger from becoming extinct. He's had a marvelous second life at a thing he was good at and loved.

Of course there are some people who leave advertising agencies when they're in their 40s and 50s who really don't have any interest in any other sort of occupation. They have done advertising for a while and that's what they like, that's what interests them. What can they do? Well, there's something I wish happened, and it never seems to happen in agencies – it doesn't happen in ours.

Off to the village on a household errand.

Let's say there's a man called Snodgrass. And he's 55. And he's rather run out of gas and he's not been contributing for some time, and so it's decided by the management that he just has to go. Some poor devil has to tell him this.

Why does he have to go? Let's say he's rather high up in the hierarchy. Lets say he's a Senior Vice President, or something very grand like that. Why can't he say to the agency: well I'm sorry you feel this way, but there it is, there's no point in arguing. But I don't want to leave. I want you to give me another job at a far lower salary. Without any title. I want to just make myself useful, in some sort of very different job. I might be good at that.

Then he would be able to keep in touch with all his friends at the agency, keep in touch with the advertising business, not suffer so badly as you do when you're separated.

Some people would worry about the loss of face.

Yeah, but there are worse things than loss of face. Like staying home and having absolutely nothing to do and no interest in life and being lonely, out of touch with all the people you like, and so forth.

Most founders of companies either hang on too long, like Leo Burnett, or retire and detach themselves entirely, like Raymond Rubicam. You've done neither. How have you sustained your interest at such a high level for so long a time with so little direct control?

I don't know. I *have* sustained my interest. I think I'm just as interested in advertising now as I ever was.

I love the interest, it's a big thing in my life. I'm also not indifferent to the salary. I get a salary. You may think that's scandalous, but I do. It's not one of the biggest salaries in the company, but it's a reasonable, fair thing.

Let's talk a little about losing direct control. That is often a great frustration for me. Because there are times when I wish I could control things and I can't. There's an old French saying: *He who is absent is always wrong.* And I'm wrong. Some of the decisions I deplore have been taken when I wasn't at the meeting. Because I'm in France, and the meetings are mostly in New York. So I've lost arguments which otherwise I might have won if I'd been there.

What bugs you?

Bullies. (I'm not sure that I'm not a frightful bully myself.)

Bores. Above all bores. I think boring is the ultimate sin.

Creative people who refuse to study the product or the research or to admit there's more than one way to skin a cat.

Incompetence in the advertising business. I look at an ad or commercial, all too many of the commercials in fact, and I say that is just an incompetent piece of work. The guy doesn't know what he's doing.

You know what I mean there? It's not a question of philosophy of advertising. I'm not arguing about that. *Whatever* he's trying to do, he doesn't know how to do it. He's incompetent. He doesn't know his trade. He's an amateur.

What do you look for in young people that suggests leadership potential?

This is a very, very difficult question. I was having diner with the McKinsey partners a few years ago, and I asked them that question. I said, you know a lot about leadership in business, how do you identify a leader?

They said, ah, that's the thing you never know. The only

thing that may be true is that people who have been leaders when they were in school quite often turn out to be leaders in mature life.

But on the whole leadership seems to be unpredictable. It's a very serious problem for businesses.

Were you able to spot our leaders early on or were you surprised by who emerged?

I wasn't able to spot them.

Who's the most stimulating person you've ever met?

I think one of the most stimulating people I've ever known was and still is Teodoro Moscoso, the great Puerto Rican head of the Economic Department for Puerto Rico. I've always found him intensely stimulating. At least he stimulated me and got very good work out of me.

Can you expand on that? Was it the play of his mind? His energy?

Well, I can give you an example.

One thing that I found very stimulating is that he *did* things. He got things done. I've known a lot of people in different governments and businesses who really couldn't get anything to happen, but he made things happen.

His job was to get industry to Puerto Rico because they'd got terrible unemployment, poverty. And the campaign went very well. He built up a good department. One day, about three years later, I said to him, Ted, you know this thing of yours in Puerto Rico is going very well, but you watch out because if you keep on going out and getting industry and factories on that beautiful island, it's going to come to be sort of like Detroit. Do you really want that to happen?

He said, well, what do you suggest?

I said, I'll tell you what I suggest. My native land is Scotland and that was regarded around the world as a barbaric country without any culture until a refugee from Berlin called Rudolf Bing went to Edinburgh and started the Edinburgh Festival of music and drama. Within about two years, Edinburgh had become a place of pilgrimage of cultured people from all over the world.

Moscoso took out one of our agency pocket diaries we gave away at Christmas and made a little note on it. Within six months, he persuaded Pablo Casals to go and live in Puerto Rico and start the Puerto Rico Music Festival, the Casals Festival they called it.

At the end of a long interview, a tedious reporter asked Abe Burrows, the musical comedy writer, what the low point of his life had been. Burrows replied "I hate to say, kid, but I think this is it." What irritates you most about interviews?

Being interviewed by an individual who doesn't know anything about the subject.

The best interview I ever had was on the Larry King Show, a Washington radio program, Washington D.C. I told several other interviewers I was going to be done by him and they said he's the best interviewer on the air. And so he is.

The interview was on my book. I arrived in his studio at midnight. It was immediately apparent that Larry King hadn't opened the book he was about to interview me on. It didn't matter in the least. He started reading the book and asking me questions as he went along. Nobody could see this, it was just radio.

In about two minutes he had me up and running. The interview took from midnight until three in the morning. He was simply fantastic.

I said afterwards you're the best of all interviewers. What is your secret? He said: *An absolute ungovernable curiosity.*

Another thing about interviewing, you can't control what comes out in an interview. You're always frightened what words they're going to put in your mouth, and I'm afraid of indiscretion. When I was young and flighty, in the early days of Ogilvy & Mather, I used to be very outspoken in my interviews. That was one of the reasons I was always being interviewed. They could always get good quotes from me.

I wasn't afraid of offending clients then. Now I'm terrified of it. I'm terrified of saying something which will annoy a client very much. Or upset the stock market or something. I've got much more cautious. Therefore duller than I used to be. Not so exciting in an interview.

Are there any other questions you wish I had asked?

To what do you owe your success?

You wish I'd asked, to what do you owe your success?

Yes.

David, to what do you owe your success?

The fashionable answer to that is to say luck. Pure luck. That's what modest people say. They don't want to say I owe my success to my ineffable genius.

It has absolutely nothing to do with luck. Everybody's equally lucky. I don't believe in luck.

It was William James, wasn't it, who referred to success as the bitch goddess in a letter to H.G. Wells? I was talking at my old school not long ago in Scotland and I gave them a little sermon on the subject of success. They should stop thinking about success entirely in terms of material achievements and careers and all that stuff and think of success in terms of their own happiness and the happiness of their family and so on.

To what do I owe my material success? First of all, I'm the most objective man who ever lived, including objective about myself.

Second, I'm a very, very hard worker. I really work very hard when I'm doing a job. I put a lot into it.

Next thing is I'm a good salesman. I used to be good at getting new business. That's terribly important. It's under-estimated in the advertising business now – getting new business. Most people in advertising don't know anything about it. They go to work in an agency. They're given an account or a group of accounts that some joker got a few years ago. The bed is ready made for them.

I had to make my own bed. I was a very, very good salesman. I don't know why. But I was a good salesman. And that's an important thing to be.

I had a reasonably original mind, but not too much so. Which helped, not being too original. I thought as clients think. I also thought as women think. One of the advertising directors of Lever Brothers, who left, came to see me to say goodbye, and said David you're very good at selling things to women. And the reason is, I've thought a lot about it, the reason is you are a woman. You think as women think. So that's another thing.

I had a terrific advantage when I started an agency in New York. I had an English accent. With so many agencies, so much competition, I'd got a gimmick – my English accent which helped to differentiate me from the ordinary. There are an awful lot of English over there in advertising now, but in those days there were only about two of us. That was very helpful.

I've always had an eye for the main chance. I've made a lot of speeches and written a lot of talks to different audiences and I'm always selling Ogilvy & Mather. I hope I conceal that sometimes, but I am. The things are loaded with commercials for the agency.

I once went to a lunch, a thing called the Scottish Council. They had a lunch in New York. They were a small group of Scotsmen and got together. There were about ten people. And I smelled billing. And from that lunch I eventually got Shell, because Max Burns, the then President of Shell, was at the lunch. I got Thom McAn shoes because the man who owned Thom McAn shoes was at the lunch. I got British Travel, because Jim Turbayne, head of BTA, New York, was there. And one other. I forget which. All from one lunch. I can smell billing.

Also – this is related to being objective – I came into advertising from research and that gave me great advantage. I always approached the creative role, I'd see the creative thing, through a researcher's eyes. I'm almost unique in that. Very few creative people do. A lot of creative people fight research and don't want much to do with it. I was the exact opposite. I came at it from research and suddenly I was doing very good campaigns. And that gave me great advantage I think. It was unique. Still is.

And for a time, I had a short period in my life, I think maybe ten years at the outside, when I was pretty close to being a genius and I can look back on that with interested curiosity and affection and some nostalgia. Then it ran out. But I was. I was creating most of the campaigns myself. And I was doing a lot of other things.

If you asked me what my biggest achievement in Ogilvy & Mather has been, I think I'd say new business. I'd put it ahead of creative. I made a calculation of all the accounts I'd personally brought in – I always went off to new accounts alone, I didn't like doing it as a team – and I totted up all the money they've given us since I've brought them in. If in the beginning, instead of taking a salary, I'd taken one percent of the billing I brought in, I would have made four times as much money over the years as I did make.

Take Shell. How did you do it? You say it started when you went to that lunch and smelled billings. What would you do? You wouldn't just go up to Max Burns and start selling the agency, would you?

Well, this Scottish Council, when I smelled the billings, I joined it. We'd have lunch once about every two months together. We'd talk about business and getting this or that for Scotland and so on.

And Max Burns used to come to lunch quite a lot. Then we would somehow talk about advertising at lunch. And one day he decided to fire his agency. It was J. Walter Thompson. He'd had them for something like 30 years. He set up a committee to pick the new agency. There were four candidates and he put Ogilvy & Mather on the list.

The committee sent all the agencies a questionnaire. I never answered questionnaires, they irritated me. But this time I did. About 25 questions. But I knew that committee wasn't really going to pick that agency. I knew that Max Burns was going to pick it. And I couldn't reach him. 'Cause he was in London.

So I went to London. And he was staying at Claridge's. And I called Claridge's and he never called back. I was pretty desperate. Finally, the day before he left he called me back. I said Max, I'm having lunch at the House of Commons today with the Secretary of State for Scotland. Would you like to join us? He said, I'd love to. So he came to lunch.

After lunch we were walking back to my hotel, it's pouring with rain, he hadn't got an umbrella, and I had, so I kept him dry. He was grateful for that. I was able to tell him during that walk all the points I'd made in answering the questionnaire. That was very important. But more than anything else what got us the Shell account was the Rolls-Royce campaign. He thought that was a very intelligent piece of work. It was only $100,000 a year, but it got us the huge Shell account.

You went to London just to see Max Burns?

Yeah.

I suppose you had a few other things to do there too?

Nothing. Just waited. Chewing my fingernails.

Afterwards I went back to America. I went on holiday, in Massachusetts, and forgot about it. Then one day the telephone rang, it was Monty Spaght, calling from Shell to tell me we'd got it. And I said God help me. And he thought that was a very peculiar reaction.

But what I meant was I thought it was a damned difficult job and God help me to do it properly.

Chronology of
David Mackenzie Ogilvy

Born at West Horsley in England, June 23, 1911.

Fettes College, Edinburgh, 1924–1929.

Christ Church, Oxford, 1929–1931.

Chef at Hotel Majestic Paris, 1931.

Salesman for Aga Cookers, Scotland, 1932–1935.

Joined Mather & Crowther in London, 1935.

Went to United States to study American advertising for Mather & Crowther, 1938.

Associate Director of Dr. George Gallup's Audience Research Institute, Princeton, 1939–1942.

With British Security Coordination, Washington, D.C., 1942–1944.

Second Secretary, British Embassy, 1944–1945.

Farmer in Lancaster County, Pennsylvania, 1946–1948.

Co-founded Hewitt, Ogilvy, Benson & Mather, New York, 1948.

Board of Directors, New York Philharmonic, 1957–1967.

Chairman, Public Participation Committee for Lincoln Center, 1958–1960.

Trustee, Colby College, 1962–1969.

Wrote *Confessions of an Advertising Man* (1963), *Blood, Brains & Beer* (1978), *Ogilvy on Advertising* (1983).

Commander of the British Empire, 1967.

Chairman, United Negro College Fund, 1968.

Moved to France, 1973.

Trustee, World Wildlife Fund International, since 1975.

Worldwide Creative Head, Ogilvy & Mather (after retirement as Chairman), 1975–1983.

AAF Advertising Hall of Fame (in the US), 1976.

Honorary Doctor of Letters, Adelphi University, 1977.

Active in company affairs as Founder and Director, 1983–1995.

Non-executive Chairman of WPP Group after takeover by WPP, 1989–1992.

Officer, Ordre des Arts & Letters, French government, 1990.

Dies aged 88, at his home, Chateau de Touffou, 1999.

Credits

The photographs in this book come from the Ogilvy family and the Ogilvy Group, Inc., with the exception of the following:

The excerpt from the interview on page 35 is reprinted by permission of Svante Löforgen and *Resume*.